# Competition in American Politics
## An Economic Model

# Competition in American Politics

## An Economic Model

**Andrew M. Scott**
The University of North Carolina

HOLT, RINEHART AND WINSTON, INC.
*New York   Chicago   San Francisco*
*Atlanta   Dallas   Montreal   Toronto   London   Sydney*

1  2  3  4  5  6  7  8  9
Printed in the United States of America

# Preface

Competition is a central feature of the American political system. Curiously, however, the analysis of political competition has not been a matter of interest to many political scientists and a mature theory of political competition has never been developed. Because a usable theory of political competition did not exist, the author fell into the habit of using economic terminology to describe competitive political phenomena. Others have adopted the same practice. Public relations specialists talk of "selling" a particular candidate or question whether voters will "buy" a given candidate or party position. The author came to perceive that this practice was not purely inadvertent but represented an unconscious recognition of an important feature of the American political system, the role of political exchange.

Instead of relying upon economic analogy in a casual way, the author decided to make a systematic examination of the applicability of economic ideas to the study of political competition. Economists have long been concerned with competition and have developed an elaborate body of doctrine to assist in its analysis. If politics involves competition—as it does—then the analytic concepts developed by economists to deal with competition should prove applicable to the study of politics. Thus far the marriage appears to be a happy one.

This volume is an extended analytic essay on political competition, political markets, and political exchange. It does not seek to offer new knowledge, in the strict sense of the term, but to formulate new questions and to restate familiar questions in a new way. The need for a new approach to the study of the American political system seems evident. If existing perspectives had the capacity to generate integrated whole-system insights, it seems likely that they would have revealed that capacity by now. The shortage of powerful theoretical insights into the functioning of the political system as a whole speaks strongly to the need for exploring new avenues of attack.

In recent years a number of scholars have become interested in applying economic analysis to noneconomic social behavior. My debt to these writers will be evident throughout the book. Robert A. Dahl and Charles E. Lindblom used the concept of exchange in *Politics, Economics, and Welfare*. This concept is also central to Alfred Kuhn's *The Study of Society: A Unified Approach* and Peter M. Blau's *Exchange and Power in Social Life*. R. L. Curry, Jr. and L. L. Wade in their splendid volume, *A Theory of Political Exchange: Economic Reasoning in Political Analysis*, suggest that political scientists will increasingly come to think about politics in terms of political exchange.

Anthony Downs's important study, *An Economic Theory of Democracy*, stresses the importance of competition in political markets, and Charles Lindblom's *The Intelligence of Democracy* emphasizes the role of the market as a coordinating device. Others who have contributed importantly to the development of a new interest in political economy are James Buchanan, Gordon Tullock, Kenneth Arrow, Duncan Black, and William Riker. William C. Mitchell and Joyce M. Mitchell have written a very interesting introductory text devoted to this approach, *Political Analysis and Public Policy: An Introduction to Political Science*.

Work on this book began a number of years ago but has been intermittent; the author's first notes to himself on the relevance of oligopoly theory to party competition date back to 1954. A first draft of the manuscript was completed and placed in the hands of the publishers in February, 1968. During the ensuing months the manuscript was reworked but without significant modification of its central ideas. The formulations offered here are necessarily first approximations, and the author has been willing to run the risk of occasional oversimplification in the interest of seeing how far selected economic analogies could be pushed.

The Faculty Research Council of the University of North Carolina supported work on this volume with a research grant, and I should like to express my gratitude for that assistance.

Andrew M. Scott

Chapel Hill, North Carolina
December 1969

# Contents

# Contents

# Chapter One
# The Political Market and Political Exchange

A democratic society, such as that found in the United States, must find ways to make a great many decisions–decisions pertaining to roads, dams, national defense, national parks, health services, flood control, air safety, agricultural policy, tariff policy, health services, police protection, and so on. It must not only make decisions on these matters but the decisions must be related to the needs and wants of the persons affected by them. Finally, the decisions, when made, must be accepted as legitimate by individuals in the society. These are not easy conditions to satisfy but they can be met if collective decisions are made within the framework of a political market.

Political markets play a central role in the functioning of the American political system since they provide the means by which the system produces many of its most important decisions. In a properly functioning market virtually any issue can be translated into terms that will allow individuals to pass on it: Should a school bond be approved and should a sewer bond be turned down? Should the city modify its form of government? Should Mr. $X$ or Mr. $Y$ be elected to Congress? The political market allows individuals to choose from among competing individuals, organizations, and programs and as a consequence of their choice governments are established, men are placed in office or removed from office, decisions are made pertaining to foreign policy, the quality of national life, the allocation of scarce resources, and the rules governing the functioning of the political system itself (changes in voting age, modification of the electoral college, and so on).

In a large market there will be many individuals and many issues on which they have preferences. The mechanism of the marketplace collects these multitudinous preferences into a manageable number of comprehensible political outcomes or decisions. Out of the turmoil of the marketplace a handful of decisions emerge which are customarily accepted as legitimate expressions of societal preference. This is what makes the political market so remarkable an institution. By its alchemy the expression of purely individual preference is converted into collective decisions. "In an effectively democratic political order, collective decisions emerge from a process that takes individual expressions of preference as inputs and somehow combines these to produce outcomes."[1] These collective decisions are made without collective agreement and yet are accepted as legitimate and authoritative for society as a whole. They are accepted as legitimate not because of their content but because of the way they are made. The market process makes democracy workable. Without it, it would not be possible to offer a viable alternative to authoritarian decision-making.[2]

As decision-making systems, economic markets and political markets have a good deal in common.

> In a capitalist democracy there are essentially two methods by which social choices can be made: voting, typically used to make "political" decisions, and the market mechanism, typically used to make "economic" decisions. . . . The methods of voting and the market . . . are methods of amalgamating the tastes of many individuals in the making of social choices.[3]

[1]James Buchanan, *Public Finance in Democratic Process* (Chapel Hill: University of North Carolina Press, 1967), p. 144.

[2]The normal working of the system is being discussed here. Under certain circumstances decisions made in the political market will not be generally accepted as legitimate. Official United States policy regarding Viet Nam war generated widespread discontent and protest, for example.

[3]Kenneth Arrow, *Social Choice and Individual Values* (New York: John Wiley, 1951), pp. 1–2.

The kind of choice that an individual is concerned with in a political market will usually be different from the kind he is concerned with in an economic market.[4] In an economic market he is typically concerned with private goods while in a political market he is more likely to be concerned with public goods. In one he will exchange his resources for a television set, a car, or a swimming pool while in the other he will give his support in order to improve the prospects of a particular candidate or public policy. In both cases he is exchanging something for something else. The individual cannot "own" an antipollution ordinance in the same way that he can own a new Ford, but each may have value to him and he may be prepared to expend resources (time, energy, money, influence) in order to obtain both of them.[5]

A political market has several identifying characteristics: It has physical extension; buyers and sellers are active in it; buyers and sellers engage in exchange behavior; exchange behavior is governed by certain rules; terms of exchange are influenced by supply and demand.

The basic processes of such a market are simple. Sellers (who may be individuals or organizations) are engaged in the marketing of political products. These products may include candidates, programs, pledges, ideological stands, legislative action, past accomplishments, and so on. Sellers compete for the attention of buyers (who also may be individuals or organizations). A candidate seeking office tries to "sell" himself, his party, and a set of programs and attitudes to his constituents. He may also pledge to do various things in return for their support. "Vote for me and I will push the interests of this District when I am elected to Congress." The candidate or political organization wants support and offers a program designed to attract that support.

[4]For an examination of selected collective decision models see James Buchanan, *Public Finance in Democratic Process* (Chapel Hill: University of North Carolina Press, 1967), Chapter Two.

[5]"Like considerations would apply to many of the traditional services of government, including preventive health services, maintenance of law and order, education, fire protection, beautification of the landscape, flood control and many others. The benefits from all of these goods are more or less 'indivisible' and 'social.' Consequently the provision of these goods must usually be carried on in response to *collective* rather than individual choice." Howard R. Bowen, *Toward Social Economy* (New York: Holt, Rinehart, and Winston 1948), p. 174.

The constituent, in turn, is prepared to offer his support to the individual or organization that appears most attractive to him. This support may take any number of forms: a vote, endorsement, a campaign contribution, an offer to work in his campaign, and so on. When a constituent "buys" the program offered by a candidate and supports him a transaction may be said to have taken place even though the exchange was not formal and explicit. The constituent has exchanged his support for the products offered by the candidate.

It may seem strange at first to think of constituent support as having a market value and hence of being open to market analysis but it quite obviously does have such value. It manifestly has market value because sellers are constantly engaged in competing for it and in modifying their behavior in order to attract it. That it has value is also testified to by the fact that laws are needed to prevent corruption. If votes, or other forms of support, did not have a scarcity value they could not be bought and sold.[6] The buying and selling of votes in big city elections has not been uncommon and the price that a vote will bring on the market is a function of the supply and demand situation. Legislative bribery is uncommon but the basic exchange process is the same. To cite a classic example: In Albany during the famed Erie War, Jay Gould apparently bought legislative votes in substantial numbers. The size of the bribe varied with the influence of the legislator involved.[7] The process of vote-trading or logrolling also gives evidence of the exchange value of legislative votes.

[6]"The economic value of votes is confirmed by the selling and buying activities of individuals in 'corrupt' circumstances. . . . There seems to have been present a rather common failure to recognize the simple fact that if political votes did not have economic value, 'corruption' would be impossible." James Buchanan and Gordon Tullock, *The Calculus of Consent: Logical Foundations of Constitutional Democracy* (Ann Arbor: University of Michigan Press, 1962), p. 121.

[7]"He (Jay Gould) dealt in large sums. He gave to one man, in whom he said 'he did not take much stock,' the sum of $5,000, 'just to smooth him over.' This man had just before received $5,000 of Erie money from another agent of the company. It would, therefore, be interesting to know what sums Mr. Gould paid to those individuals in whom he did 'take much stock.' Another individual is reported to have received $100,000 from one side, 'to influence legislation,' and to have subsequently received $70,000 from the other side to disappear with the money; which he accordingly did, and thereafter became a gentleman of elegant

Market processes revolve around exchange. Exchange theory, therefore, is an important analytic instrument in the study of markets. Exchange involves giving one thing in order to obtain another. What an actor in the market gives up represents the cost of the exchange to him and what he receives is the reward from the exchange. Exchange will normally occur when the costs to each actor are more than offset by the rewards that each expects to get. In a voluntary exchange each party expects to gain, otherwise the exchange would not take place. Nothing guarantees that each party must benefit equally however.

Before two parties can engage in an exchange each must determine how much of one commodity is worth how much of another. In other words, the terms must be established. In economic markets the terms of exchange are usually expressed by means of a price. If a candy bar "costs" ten cents this means that the proprietor of a store will exchange the candy bar for ten cents. A political market is a nonprice market however so the value of a commodity will not be expressed in dollars and cents. It is akin to a market in which bartering takes place. In such a market the value of a commodity will be expressed in terms of the amount of another resource that it can command in the marketplace. For example, if $1X$ can be exchanged for $2Y$, this ratio may be thought of as the "price" of $X$. In this example $X$ might represent a political product, such as a promise to increase social security or a promise to provide law and order.

If the exchange value of a product increases, suppliers of that product will normally stand ready to increase the supply in the market. The result might be a supply curve having the following appearance. As the value of $X$ increases, however, consumers will seek to use it more sparingly since they will have to give up more

---

leisure. One senator was openly charged in the columns of the press with receiving a bribe of $20,000 from one side, and a second bribe of $15,000 from the other. . . . Other senators were blessed with a sudden accession of wealth, but in no case was there any jot or tittle of proof of bribery. Mr. Gould's rooms at the Devlin House overflowed with a joyous company, and his checks were numerous and heavy; but why he signed them, or what became of them, he seemed to know less than any man in Albany." Charles Francis Adams, Jr., "A Chapter of Erie," in *Chapters of Erie* by Charles Francis Adams, Jr., and Henry Adams (Ithaca: Cornell University Press, 1956), p. 53.

to get it. As its price drops, on the other hand, they will be prepared to consume more of it. A demand curve for $X$ is shown in the figure below.

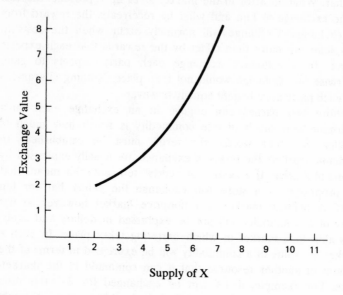

Supply of X

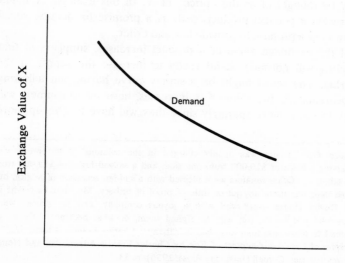

Demand for X

If the exchange value of $X$ should become stabilized, then supply and demand might find an equilibrium point as in the figure below. At exchange value $OV$ supply and demand are in equilibrium and amount $OH$ will be offered on the market.

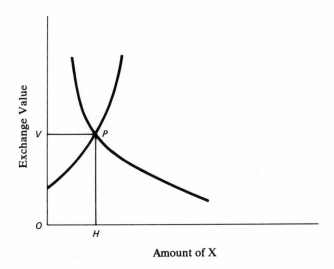

Amount of X

The more scarce a product is relative to demand the greater will be its price in terms of other resources which it can command. This holds in political markets as well as in economic markets. For example, since skilled political public relations experts are scarce their services command generous pay. A firm specializing in that type of work will have a strong bargaining position and may be able to insist not only on high pay but on a high degree of control over the campaign of the candidate or party that seeks to employ it.

If the demand for a product is high, and returns on resources used for it are high, new means may be devoted to that use. To continue the example above, additional firms may begin to engage in political public relations work. This would move the supply curve to the right and the exchange value of this type of service would decline. In time a new equilibrium might be achieved at $P^2$ as indicated in the next figure. Conversely, if demand for a product is weak relative to supply, the returns to that use of resources will drop and, in time, less of the product will be offered on the market. This would shift the supply curve to the left and the price of that product would increase.

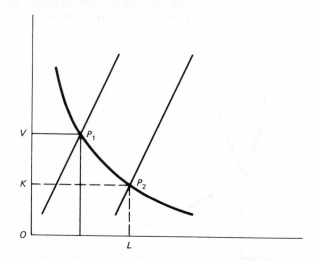

Frequently demand and supply are both variables and the process is one of mutual adjustment by means of successive approximations. The process of adjustment may be jerky, imperfect, may involve a substantial time lag, and may never be consummated. The elasticity of supply and the elasticity of demand will have a great influence on the adjustment process.

There is much to be learned about supply and demand relationships in political markets. What factors affect the supply of a particular product and how do these factors vary from one product to the next? What circumstances would lead to a shift in the location of the demand curve? It is clear that changes in the state of mind of consumers might radically alter the demand picture. During an economic recession consumer demand for policies looking toward prosperity will increase. In a time of racial unrest a premium will be placed upon promising civil rights leaders, new ideas, and perhaps measures for riot control. In a time of limited war there is likely to be a ready market for programs that promise an end to the war.

# Chapter Two
# Parties and Political Competition

The Constitution was drafted without regard for political parties. The framers simply did not anticipate the coming of national political parties.

The members of the Philadelphia Convention, writing before the dawn of party government in the United States, did not understand that parties provided a way—perhaps the only way—of achieving a degree of popular control under a form of representative government. The provisions relating to the election of the President demonstrate that the framers expected the individual electors in the electoral college to decide independently upon the most qualified man without the formation and interposition of organized groups. Yet it is precisely at this point, the election of national officials, that parties are unfailingly found.

How far the framers were from an understanding of the principles of party government is made clear by their great concern for the doctrine of separation of powers. They thought it essential for the avoidance of tyranny that each branch of the government have an area in which it could function in relative independence of the others. The idea of a party victorious in an election taking over both the legislative and executive branches of government would have seemed to them the very definition of tyranny. Yet the Constitution had scarcely gone into effect before the Federalist party took recognizable form and did precisely that.[1]

The framers anticipated that there would be political competition but they did not envision that it would take the form of competition between stable national parties. Insofar as the development of political parties was foreseen at all, it was dreaded.

> Yet it seems quite safe to say that of all the institutions of modern democracy, none was so badly understood, so poorly foreseen, or, paradoxically, so dreaded in the late eighteenth century as the emergence of organized, institutionalized permanent political parties regularly competing with one another in national elections and continuing their antagonistic confrontation even between elections.[2]

Because parties have lacked an assured place in the theory of American democracy they have seemed slightly disreputable through much of American history and have received relatively little systematic attention. In fact, however, political parties are essential to democracy. Competing political parties exist in every genuine democracy. They are the instruments through which competition takes place and competition for voter support is the heart of democracy. In the absence of an appreciation for the role of political parties it has not been possible to develop an adequate theory of political competition nor, therefore, a fully rounded theory of democracy.

A party functions within a special environment, a political market. This market will have a structure and the features of the structure will have to do with the number of parties in the market, differences in their size, how actively they are competing, the nature of their collaboration, barriers to the entry of third parties, and so on. The structure of a market is important because it influences the way that the market will develop in the future and the behavior of actors in the market. For example, a highly competitive market is likely to elicit quite different behavior than a market in which the level of competition is low. Market structure also affects policy outcomes.

---

[1]Andrew M. Scott, *Political Thought in America* (New York: Holt, Rinehart and Winston, 1959), pp. 154–155.

[2]Robert A. Dahl, *Pluralist Democracy in the United States* (Chicago: Rand McNally, 1967), p. 203.

The structure of political markets is a very important point, since political outcomes will be partly, indeed largely, determined by them. That this is true is attested to by the seriousness with which some people take things like constitutions, statutes, treaties, agency regulations, and other less formal "rules of the game."[3]

The single most important feature of a market is probably the degree of competition in it. One way to approach the study of political competition is to fashion a model of perfect political competition and then to note the ways in which actual market conditions fall short of this model. Perfect political competition would appear to require the following:

1) All actors in the market, buyers and sellers alike, must have perfect knowledge of the market—such as current issues, the stands of candidates, their records, the range of options that exist.

2) This means, in turn, that all actors have to be strongly motivated, thoroughly politicized, and must be able to devote a good deal of time and energy to the pursuit of information. The significance of all information must be immediately perceived.

3) The communications system must work perfectly throughout the market. Information must be transmitted instantaneously and must reach all actors without fail.

4) Actors in the market must not let emotional attachments interfere with calculations of self-interest. This means that a political organization cannot develop an attachment to a particular program but would have to stand ready to adopt or drop programs in accordance with their popularity. The voter, in turn, cannot develop an emotional attachment to a party, a candidate, or a particular stance that would impede a choice based upon self-interest.

[3]R. L. Curry, Jr., and L. L. Wade, *A Theory of Political Exchange: Economic Reasoning in Political Analysis,* © 1968. By permission of Prentice-Hall, Inc., Englewood Cliffs, New Jersey. P. 73.

5)   There must be many buyers and sellers so that no single one can have an appreciable effect on the demand and supply situation within the market.

6)   Entry into the market and departure from it of new parties must be easy.

7)   Organizations in the market (whether producers, consumers, or distributors) must have no internal cleavages that would interfere with an immediate and purely self-interested response to a market situation.

These demanding criteria are not satisfied by political markets in the United States. Knowledge of the market is always imperfect on the part of both buyers and sellers. Interest in public affairs is often lacking and voters are frequently unwilling to bear the cost—in terms of time, energy, and expense—of becoming informed. Perfect political competition requires men to be completely political, moving unhesitatingly as their interests dictate. If men really shifted instantly in pursuit of their interests, party identification would not have the importance it has, and voters and political organizations would not exhibit the rigidity they often do in clinging to obsolete or irrelevant positions. The number of political organizations in the market is small. The ease of entry into political markets required by the model of perfect competition is patently out of accord with reality. In practice, it is hard for a new political party to enter a market and the larger the market the more difficult is the entry. Established parties are likely to have a hold on the loyalties of voters, to have access to funds, and to have an organizational apparatus that cannot be easily duplicated in a short period of time. Fledgling parties operate at an extreme disadvantage and it is no accident that the persistence of a new party on the national scene is almost unknown. For all of these reasons, the competition that usually exists in political markets falls far short of satisfying the requirements for "perfect" competition.

The typical situation in an American political market involves only a few sellers. The relevant economic model, therefore, is not that of perfect competition but that of oligopoly.

The four basic characteristics of an oligopoly are as follows: (1) several entities share control of the market—each entity sets its own exchange ratio according to its own view of the market, and each entity determines its own output; (2) each entity offers an output that is somehow distinguishable from the outputs of other entities; (3) it is difficult for new entities to enter the market because of the existence of restricted access; and, (4) there is usually imperfect knowledge of the market.[4]

More precisely, a market is usually dominated by *two* parties, which automatically suggests the relevance of the theory of duopoly. "The duopoly case has a wide range of applicability in politics."[5] The model of duopolistic competition illuminates the entire matter of two-party competition in the United States. Under conditions of perfect competition, as noted earlier, the behavior of one party would not have an appreciable effect on the behavior of other parties. Under the conditions of a duopoly, however, each organization controls a relatively large proportion of the total market. Interdependence, instead of being negligible, may be the most important factor that each party has to consider. Neither party can control or even predict fully what the other will do, yet each must base its own behavior on calculations about the intentions of the other.

In this situation of interdependence, the two parties will have conflicting interests but it is easy to see that they may also have interests in common. If each party were to communicate certain kinds of information to the other the uncertainty and risk for both would be reduced. Political parties normally expect to compete with one another, but they have a shared interest in competing in accordance with certain rules of the game. From the point of view of party leaders, an orderly, restrained competition may have much to recommend it. It makes for a more pleasant existence if the game is played in such a way that one's errors are not penalized by personal disgrace nor by the lasting ruin of one's party.

A political market will typically be characterized by a mixture of competitive behavior and collaborative behavior. It is helpful to think of a spectrum of possible mixes of collaboration and competition ranging from pure competition at one extreme to pure collaboration at the other.

[4]Curry and Wade, p. 85. The discussion in Chapter 4, "Exchange Conditions in Political Market Structures" is helpful.
[5]Curry and Wade, p. 86.

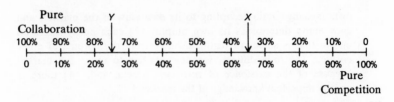

Any example of duopoly can be located on some point along this scale. In a market designated by point *X*, 65 percent of the behavior of the parties could be explained in terms of competition and 35 percent in terms of collaboration. This would mean that two parties, while competing vigorously in some respects nevertheless collaborate in certain others. At point *Y*, 75 percent of party behavior would be explained in terms of collaboration while only 25 percent could be explained in terms of competition. This would probably mean that the two parties had come to an understanding and that the leaders of the smaller party were content that their party should remain in a minority position. Unless a market is 100 percent competitive, elements of collaboration will remain and unless a market is 100 percent collaborative, elements of competition will remain.

If little systematic attention has been given to political competition even less has been lavished upon political collaboration. Yet market collaboration between parties that are putative opponents is common and persistent and needs to be recognized and explained. From the point of view of the working of the American political system it is just as important to understand political collaboration as to understand political competition. A mature theory of political competition must be able to explain both and to explain the way that each is related to the other.

The circumstances of the market and the payoffs in the market will influence the extent to which parties compete or collaborate. If both parties perceive the situation as one in which only one party can survive, or as one in which the objectives of one party are absolutely unacceptable to the other, the prospects for collaboration will be poor. Game theorists would describe such a situation as a zero-sum game, a game in which the gain to one side is offset by an equal loss to the other side. If party *A* wins the governorship in a state, party *B must* lose, and there are probably no second prizes worth mentioning. In a true zero-sum game, conflict is the only reasonable strategy. Since the conflicting parties have no interests in common, no purpose is served by collaboration.

In a market that involves variable sum games, on the other hand, collaboration is likely to be found. When actors are interdependent and the payoff to each actor is dependent upon the behavior of the other, the case for collaboration is strong.[6] In such a market, political parties will have conflicting interests but will also have interests in common. If their policies are to reflect the full range of their interests they must be competitive in some respects and collaborative in other respects.

In a political market, as in an economic market, it is natural for producers to try to control the market to as great an extent as possible. If they can reduce the freedom of action of those with whom they deal they reduce the uncertainty and the risk to themselves. If two parties share a market they have an obvious common interest in discouraging the entry of a third party into that market. Such success as a third party might have could only be at their expense. Therefore, in addition to the normal obstacles that a third party would have to overcome, the dominant parties might establish others, such as making it difficult for a third party to get its name on the ballot.[7]

Collaborative behavior in a market is sometimes difficult to discern because the outward forms of political competition—nominations, campaigns, elections—are likely to be retained even though the results of these exercises may be foreordained. Collaborative behavior is often found in markets characterized by a substantial imbalance in the strength of the contending organizations. It is so common, in fact, that it may be worthwhile for an observer to look for an informal understanding whenever an imbalance between parties is stabilized at the same level for a long period of time. If the imbalance is too extreme, of course, the dominant organization would have nothing to gain by making

---

[6]Buchanan and Tullock in *The Calculus of Consent: Logical Foundations of Constitutional Democracy* (Ann Arbor: University of Michigan Press, 1962) have emphasized the nonzero-sum characteristics of certain kinds of political exchanges.

[7]For a discussion of political exclusion, see E. S. Schattschneider, *Party Government* (New York: Holt, Rinehart and Winston, 1960), Chapter V.

concessions to the smaller organization. In such a case duopoly would have been replaced by an effective monopoly and the interdependence characteristic of duopoly would have disappeared.

Collaboration appears more frequently in restricted markets—cities, states, congressional districts—than in the national market. This is easily explained in terms of what has already been said. Presidential elections have the characteristics of zero-sum games since only one party can win the big prize and the difference between winning and losing may shape events in both parties for years to come. In more restricted markets, however, there may be a variety of payoffs and this makes it easier to find a basis for collaboration. For example, the competing factions within a dominant political organization in a city might agree on a formula according to which the mayoral nomination would go to the leading faction while the opposing faction would be permitted to name the candidate for district attorney. In a state-wide contest in a one-party state, the same logic might apply to the nominations for governor and lieutenant governor. In a congressional district in a one-party state, there may be some general understanding concerning the counties from which candidates are to be nominated. If the retiring incumbent has come from the eastern part of the district, it may be understood that communities in the western part will be allowed to nominate his successor. Or, if the incumbent came from a large city, it may be understood that his successor shall come from one of the small towns. Attempts to breach understandings of this kind may generate sharp conflict and deep bitterness. The breach would endanger the basis of collaboration, which might have been hard-won, and would threaten to replace collaboration with genuine political competition.

Collaboration may take the form of a market-sharing arrangement. The leaders of the dominant party might conclude that seeking a larger portion of the market would force the minority party into greater activity in self-defense. They might also decide that gaining a few percentage points in an election was not worth the effort involved, might open them to charges of being dictatorial, and might lead to increased factionalism in the party. The leaders of the minority party might be quite content with their modest portion of the market if they felt they had no chance of winning the election regardless of the effort they put out. Why should they exhaust themselves in order to lose by a slightly reduced margin? Furthermore, they might calculate that their control of the party would be endangered if they competed more actively and attracted substantial numbers of new adherents. The leaders in both parties might therefore conclude, quite rationally, that they were better off under the present arrangements than if active competition made interparty relationships fluid and uncertain.

In the Southern states, long dominated by the Democratic party, Republican party leaders have often been content not to engage in real competition. The absence of a grass roots Republican party has not always been a source of regret to them. It is easier to control a languid party than an active one and if the party remained dormant there was no threat to their position as official leaders of the Republican party in the state. This position guaranteed that they would be wooed by the national Republican leadership because of their convention votes. Furthermore, they may have felt that their individual positions in the community would be jeopardized if the Republican party ever became a real threat to Democratic dominance. In these circumstances it is quite understandable that they should choose to engage only in *pro forma* competition and that their tacit collaboration with the Democrats should be stable and long-lived.

The stability of this arrangement would be threatened if it should appear to a segment of Republican leadership that they might actually have a chance to win. In this case there would probably be a contest for control of the state Republican party between the old guard, on the one hand, and new leadership committed to genuine political competition on the other. This is a pattern that has emerged, for example, in North Carolina.

Sometimes parties collaborate by agreeing tacitly not to raise a particular issue. By their behavior the leaders of each party say to the leaders of the other party, "I have not raised this issue and do not plan to do so unless you raise it first." This type of collaboration would be a rational response to a situation in which neither set of leaders could be confident of the electoral outcome if a volatile issue were raised. It is symmetrical collaboration in the sense that each party offers the other a *quid pro quo*.

Under some circumstances a minority party might be willing to accept a form of issue leadership from the majority party. That is, it might be content to operate within the frame of reference established by the majority party and not raise issues that the majority party had not already raised. This would be asymmetrical collaboration since no *quid pro quo* was received from the other organization. In this example the minority party chooses not to compete but the majority party makes no corresponding concession.

Economists are accustomed to observing that firms in a market may engage in nonprice competition. In much the same way political organizations may engage in peripheral or nonsubstantive forms of competition. Instead of competing in the realm of policy and program, competition may be confined to public relations activity and the "politics of personality." Political competition in the one party states of the South have often exemplified the politics of personality. In such cases candidates do not conduct a search for new issues but are content to make minor changes in the "packaging" of their product. Instead of seeking a genuine differentiation of their product from other products, party leaders are content to rely on minor stylistic changes.[8]

Competing political organizations or candidates are sometimes able to agree, usually tacitly, on the vigor with which a campaign is to be prosecuted and on the techniques that will not be used. Two busy men competing for a single seat on the town council might find it easy to agree to avoid expensive campaign activities such as the use of television spots. They will continue to compete but at a low level of intensity. The more intense and expensive the campaign the greater will be the loss to each man. The man who loses the election will have lost his time, his money, and the election. The victor will also be less well-off because he will have had to spend more to win than was strictly necessary.

Coordination in a market may be "horizontal" or "vertical" depending on whether the coordination involves like or unlike organizations. If two political parties coordinate their actions that is horizontal coordination. It is not restricted to producers of

---

[8]To be sure, a failure on the part of a political organization to use the full range of competitive techniques does not necessarily imply collaboration. An organization having limited resources might choose to concentrate its resources on those techniques having the greatest promise and to set others aside.

political products but may be found among consumers as well. For example an alliance of business interests might be very influential in a town. Horizontal coordination may evolve into "vertical" coordination, that is, coordination between consumers and producers. This evolution is understandable since those who control one side of a market are often in a position, if they so desire, to gain control of the other side as well.

Those who do not like the coordination existing in a given market are likely to charge collusion. As a rule, however, political collaboration across party lines is not based on formal agreement but on tacit understanding. It is not surprising that the leaders of two organizations, faced with a common problem, should arrive independently at complementary conclusions concerning appropriate strategy. The condition of the market may force the leaders of both parties to similar conclusions and so may the dynamics of their own interaction. Suppose that party *A* and party *B* have been competing in a particular political market for a number of years and the leaders of each party realize that if one spends approximately the same amount on the campaign as the other support will be divided about equally between the two. Each party realizes that if it can increase its spending unilaterally, without the other party following suit, it will be able to generate far more support than it otherwise would. The payoff matrix for this situation is shown in the figure below.

If each party has been spending $5 million on its campaign, the leaders of party *B* can see that if they double their expenditures they will receive 60 percent of the vote (cell 2) instead of merely 50 percent (cell 1). Therefore, boldly, they increase their expenditures to $10 million. The leaders of party *A*, perceiving what *B* is doing and aware of the contents of the payoff matrix, decide that they must try to match *B*'s effort (cell 5). The leaders of *B*, meanwhile, have become attached to the notion of a decisive victory over *A* and to their image of themselves as men who think big. Therefore, when they learn that *A* is planning to double its expenditures, they decide that they will increase their effort by another $5 million (cell 6). Party *A*'s leaders, desperate and fighting for what appears to be the survival of the party, up their expenditures by another $5 million. The election takes place with each party having spent $15 million instead of the normal $5

Expenditures of Party B

million. The result? Each party gets approximately 50 percent of the votes, just as it did when it spent only $5 million! Each escalatory step seemed sensible at the time it was made, but in the end neither party gained anything and each was left nearly bankrupt.

The game might have had a different outcome. The leaders of the two parties might have talked together on the golf course or at the athletic club and agreed that escalation could only lead to financial strain. In their common interest each might have agreed to head off any efforts at escalation in his own party. This is a game which has one type of outcome if the participants proceed independently and a different type of outcome if they collaborate. If the first scenario were followed, and escalation took place, the chances are good that a lesson would be learned and that the leaders would get together before the following election. Once an initial understanding was worked out the arrangement might be stable over a period of years. If collaboration in a market has persisted over a long period of time new leaders, as they come to power, do not have to work out their own understandings but can follow the pattern of limited competition that has become traditional in the market.

Political bargaining usually involves mixed motives. Those engaging in it have interests in common, and it is these common interests which propel them toward negotiation in the first instance. They also have conflicting interests, for each participant wants to maximize his benefits and minimize his costs. Each seeks asymmetry in his own favor, giving as little as possible and getting as much as he can. If either actor is too unyielding, however, the transaction will not take place and both may be losers. This realization will incline each to accept a moderate settlement in preference to no settlement at all. The negotiation may be further complicated if the two parties calculate the cost of agreement in different terms. One participant may measure the cost of a transaction in terms of dollars while the other may be thinking in terms of alternatives forgone or political support lost. If the gap between the cost/benefit calculations of the participants is so great that it cannot be bridged by compromise, there will be no transaction.

By and large, the greater the cost of a transaction to an actor the greater the rewards that he will seek from it. If he has made a considerable investment (in terms of time, money, energy, prestige, or risk), he will seek commensurate returns. Actor $A$ may argue that the risks entailed outweigh the rewards that $B$ is offering. Actor $B$ may respond that the risks to $A$ are negligible and the rewards are substantial. He might add that the cost of giving $A$ an increased reward would be more than $A$'s support is worth. Thus $B$ might finally say to $A$: "I would like your support in the upcoming election, but it is not worth my while to try to meet your terms. Your support is not as important to me as you believe it to be."

Actor $B$ might have been applying marginal analysis. Every political resource, as well as every economic resource, is subject to diminishing returns. Actor $B$ might have been prepared to make extravagant concessions to $C$ in order to get the 20,000 votes that he believes will put him in the mayor's office. He might be prepared to make substantial, though less drastic, concessions to $D$ in order to get the next 20,000 votes that can serve as insurance. Beyond that, however, the value to him of additional increments of support drops rapidly. For that reason, perhaps, actor *A* cannot get the price for his support that he had hoped to get.

Political markets in the United States are usually oligopolistic or duopolistic but occasionally monopolistic. If there is only a single seller in a market, buyers have no recourse but to meet his terms if they are to have his product. Buyers cannot exert effective pressure upon the seller, as they could in a competitive situation, and therefore the seller need not be responsive to their demands.

Not since the days of Federalist party dominance, prior to the formation of the Jeffersonian Republican party, has a political party enjoyed anything approximating monopoly on the national scene. In the big cities, on the other hand, American history has many examples of effective monopoly. Boss William Tweed had a working political monopoly in New York City; so did Martin Lomasney in Boston, Boies Penrose in Philadelphia, Thomas J. Pendergast in Kansas City, Frank Hague in Jersey City, and Edward Crump in Memphis, to mention a few examples.[9]

Once a boss controls the production side of the market he may be able to control the market as a whole. Boss Crump was able to persuade groups of voters to cooperate with him because they had nowhere else to go and because he was in a position to reward the cooperative and punish the recalcitrant. He did not have to modify the political products that he offered to the voters in response to their changing demands because he controlled demand as well as supply. In this case of vertical integration of the market those who did not play ball with him were simply out of luck.

As types of market organization, monopoly and duopoly are analytically quite distinct. In practice, however, duopoly shades off into monopoly as one party gets progressively stronger than its opponent. The substance of monopoly can sometimes be found even though, technically speaking, an opposition party is present. Was Tammany Hall, during its great days, a monopoly? Did Boies Penrose operate a monopoly in Philadelphia? Terminology

[9]See, for example, Harold Zink, *City Bosses in the United States: A Study of Twenty Municipal Bosses* (Durham, North Carolina: Duke University Press, 1930); and Charles W. Van Devander, *The Big Bosses* (New York: Howell, Soskin, 1944).

is not particularly important provided it is recognized that in these cases the minority party became so weak that the corrective forces normally associated with duopoly ceased to work.

The same type of question arises in an examination of political machines at the state level. The Democratic party dominated the states of the South for many years just as the Republican party dominated states in northern New England and the Great Plains. Was this monopoly? One of the characteristics of a monopoly is that the monopolist is able to prevent potential competitors from entering the market. According to this criterion these examples would not qualify as monopolies nor would the Byrd machine in Virginia. Huey Long's short-lived regime in Louisiana would qualify however.

When a serious study of political market structures is undertaken a far more elaborate terminology will be needed than is now available. For example, it would clearly be helpful to have a term to describe a situation that is neither a monopoly, on the one hand, nor a genuine duopoly on the other, a situation in which two parties are active but one is clearly dominant. It might also be helpful to classify market situations in terms of the ease of entry of parties into the market.

### Ease of Entry

|  |  | Easy Entry | Difficult Entry |
|---|---|---|---|
| **Number of Parties** | One Party | **1**<br>one party,<br>easy entry | **2**<br>one party,<br>difficult entry |
|  | Two Parties | **3**<br>two parties,<br>easy entry | **4**<br>two parties<br>difficult entry |

In each of the cases indicated in this simple matrix the market situation would be different. The conditions found in cell 1 would, of course, be rare. The conditions depicted in cell 2 describe a market that is both undemocratic *and* stable. Cell 3 depicts conditions that are very favorable from the point of view of a democratically functioning market. Cell 4 depicts a market condition that satisfies one of the conditions for democracy (two parties) but does not satisfy another (ease of entry).

In the United States competition between political parties is considered as natural and inevitable as the changing of the seasons. As the analysis in this chapter suggests, however, there is reason to expect that competition will sometimes be replaced by collaboration. Under some circumstances the interests of political parties may be divergent from the interests of the political system as a whole. The individual citizen is better off and the market system as a whole functions in a more democratic way if there is lively competition among political parties—but the leaders do not always think it in their interest for their parties to compete. By the same token, the maintenance of healthy competition requires ease of entry of new parties—but the interest of existing parties discourages the entry of new ones. It is in the interest of the voter to receive information about parties, candidates, and programs that is as full and as unbiased as possible—but the immediate interest of a political party may lie in presenting incomplete and slanted information. The potential for conflict between the interests of individual political parties and the requirements of the political system as a whole deserves attention.

# Chapter Three
# Political Parties and Interest Groups

## Major Parties

The market approach illuminates the role of major parties in the American two-party system. A major party may be thought of as an organization of men who offer a selection of products to consumers in a political market in the hope that consumption of these products, as expressed in terms of voter support, will enable the party to wield influence or assume office. These products normally consist of candidates, programs, policies, perspectives, and so on. A party need not sell its products to every buyer in the market. All it must do to assume office is to persuade more consumers to buy its products than the products of the other major party.

A party grows by finding increased numbers of buyers, by drawing individuals into the routine political activity necessary to keep it alive, and by the recruitment of leaders at a variety of levels. If a party wins an election and assumes office, the leaders whom it has selected become official leaders of the governing apparatus in the market area be it national, state, or local.

The party that is defeated remains in existence and criticizes the leaders of the victorious one and its selected policies and programs in an effort to draw support away from the governing party and toward itself. By focusing attention on certain issues and problems the opposition party helps to educate the citizenry and provides a channel through which citizens can express their discontents. The objective of the opposition party is to persuade the consumers of political products to withdraw their support from one line, that is, those of the governing party, in favor of the line offered by the opposition.

The history of American political parties can be analyzed in terms of their success, or lack of success, in developing and marketing products attractive to large numbers of consumers. A party prospers when it offers products that are attractive to the market, relative to those of the other party, and it languishes when its products do not attract. Since the tastes of the market undergo continuing change, products must also change.

Parties are slow-moving organizations, however, and are rarely in a position to respond quickly to sudden changes in the market. Because adjustment to changing demand is difficult, it is natural for a party to try to ease its adjustment problems by stabilizing demand. That is, a political party will not only offer products, it will try to persuade consumers to buy them. It may engage in a major marketing program to ensure that consumers will come to demand, or will continue to demand, the products that it is prepared to offer. Under some circumstances it may be easier for a party to modify market demand than to modify its products.

The management of demand can have important consequences for the functioning of the political system as a whole, and the consequences need not be sinister. If it serves to dampen erratic shifts in demand, its contribution is valuable. Furthermore, the effective political leader is often the individual who is most successful at demand management. He tells the consumers what products they should want and then persuades them to accept those products. The capacity to manipulate demand is potentially dangerous, however, since it could undermine the democratic aspects of the market system. The problem may become more serious as public relations skills come to be used progressively more in politics.

Historically, the two parties have been fairly evenly matched, with one party achieving moderate dominance for a time before losing it to the other. The Republicans carried the presidency from 1800 through 1824.[1] The Democratic party carried it from Jackson's victory in 1828 through the election of 1856, save for Whig victories in 1840 and 1848. The Republican party once again dominated the presidency from Lincoln's election in 1860 through Hoover's election in 1928, save for the 1884, 1892, and 1912. They would have carried it in 1912 if the Republican vote had not been badly split between Taft and Theodore Roosevelt. The Democratic party returned to dominance again in 1932 and has won the presidency in every election save 1952, 1956 and 1968. In two of those years the exceedingly popular Dwight Eisenhower was a candidate and in the third the Democratic party was saddled with the Viet Nam War.[2]

Party asymmetry has been typical of the American political system, but it has been a fluctuating asymmetry rather than a progressive one. The reasons for party fluctuation are not altogether clear but part of the explanation can be perceived. For one thing, the dominant party has not used its position to try to crush the weaker party. This restraint is probably to be explained by the extent to which the "rules of the game"[3] have been internalized by party leaders and by an awareness that if either party made a serious effort to crush the other it would immediately be punished by the withdrawal of popular support. In addition, the decentralized and pluralistic nature of the market system in the United States tends to prevent the disappearance of the second party. There are many smaller markets within the large national one and in some of these the party that is weaker nationally is stronger locally. For this reason a party may lose the presidency

[1]For a discussion of shifts in party voting see V. O. Key, "A Theory of Critical Elections," *The Journal of Politics*, vol. 27 February, 1955). Angus Campbell, et al., *The American Voter*. Angus Campbell, "Voters and Elections: Past and Present," *The Journal of Politics*, vol. 64 (November, 1964), pp. 745–757. Angus Campbell, "Surge and Decline: A Study of Electoral Change" and "A Classification of the Presidential Elections" in Angus Campbell, Philip E. Converse, Warren E. Miller, and Donald E. Stokes, *Elections and the Political Order* (New York: Wiley, 1966). Also Robert A. Dahl, *Pluralist Democracy in the United States* (Chicago: Rand McNally: 1967), pp. 230–238.

[2]These swings would be less clear-cut if one examined the composition of the houses of Congress, of course.

[3]See Chapter Six.

by a substantial margin and still have a very respectable congressional delegation. In the Senate, of course, only one-third of the members are elected in any given election year which prevents rapid turnover.

After a smashing defeat or a series of defeats for one of the parties, the political process seems to set various self-correcting forces in motion. The defeated party, entrenched in certain markets and with its survival not really in doubt, begins the slow process of making a comeback. It is likely to go through the political equivalent of bankruptcy proceedings. Defeat is likely to have discredited the established leadership and a new leadership may begin to emerge. The party will be under pressure to become more adaptive and to develop new programs, policies, and personalities. As part of the process of acquiring a "new look" it is likely to borrow some of the more attractive elements of the stronger party's ideology and program.

At the same time that the weaker party is trying to adjust to defeat, the stronger party is trying to adjust to victory. Electoral success may help to produce internal differences that the weak discipline of an American party cannot overcome. The stronger party may, in time, exhaust its ideology and its program. Consumers may tire of its rhetoric and its personalities. Cumulative discontents are likely to build up in the market which are not necessarily related to actions of the stronger party but which will nevertheless work against it. The stronger party, after being in office for some years, will feel forced to justify its past behavior. To institute change and to modify existing programs may seem to its leaders a confession of past error and therefore they may hold to established programs, policies, and perspectives. When new issues emerge, as they will, the weaker party may be in a position to be more flexible and more alert in seizing these issues and in developing new policies. The weaker party may come to appear to be more in tune with the times while the stronger party seems absorbed with the remembrance of things past. These factors, combined with the delight that many Americans have in supporting the underdog and upsetting the favorite, will eventually produce a "surprise" victory. The parties may now find their positions reversed and the comeback process begins again.

Whatever the full explanation for the phenomenon of party

fluctuation it is evident that the second party, in modern times, has never been in danger of extinction. The Democrats received only 34 percent of the popular vote in 1920 and 29 percent in 1924. By 1932, however, the Democratic party elected a president and in 1936 the Republican party hit its twentieth century low of 36.5 percent of the popular vote. In the space of a decade the roles of the two parties were reversed. In 1964 the Republican party received its second lowest vote percentage of the century, 38.5 percent. Four years later the Republican presidential candidate was victorious.

The development of a precise and detailed theory of party behavior must await a systematic analysis of the functioning of political parties in various markets. Why does party $A$ behave one way in market $X$ and another way in market $Z$? Why, in the same market, do parties $A$ and $B$ behave so differently? A valuable dimension might be added to the study of American political parties if they were analyzed in terms of their market performance. A profile of a party's behavior could be prepared dealing with such matters as:

- What market or markets is the party aiming at?
- What products is it offering in each market?
- What are the characteristics of those products?
- How is the product being distributed?
- Who is consuming those products?
- How much success is the party having in its marketing program?

Parties and their behavior could be compared on the basis of such profiles and differences could be noted. The functioning of the Democratic party in a county in Mississippi or Alabama is a far cry from its behavior in Detroit. The image of a party that is presented to the voters in one locality may be quite at odds with the image of that party that its leaders are trying to project nationally. Local candidates, because of the situation in which they find themselves, may mute certain party positions, distort them, or disavow them altogether. The strategy to be pursued by a party will also be deeply influenced by whether or not it controls the presidency and the Congress.

## Minor Parties

The party system in the United States is a two-party system. The working of that system cannot be fully understood, however, without consideration of minor parties and of the role that they play. There are various kinds of minor party. The splinter party results from a conflict within one of the major parties that proves to be unresolvable; the unreconciled element splinters off. Typically this happens after a national convention which results in the nomination of a candidate considered unacceptable by a militant element in the party. Splinter parties tend to dissolve quickly, rarely outliving the election. Their members go back into the old party or cross the line into the opposition. In 1948 two elements splintered off from the Democratic party and formed the Dixiecrat party and the Progressive party. Harry Truman was elected despite this defection and the splinter parties, true to form, quickly dropped out of sight.

In 1872 liberal Republicans bolted the party and nominated Horace Greeley to run against Ulysses S. Grant, the official Republican nominee. In 1912 the Bull Moose Progressives bolted the Republican party to nominate Theodore Roosevelt. The split in the Republican vote between Taft and Roosevelt threw the election to the Democratic candidate, Woodrow Wilson. In 1924 Robert LaFollette, Sr., led a bolt of Progressives from the Republican party.

In addition to splinter parties, there are single-purpose parties, such as the Know-Nothing party, the Greenback party, and the Prohibition party. Single-purpose parties are most likely to arise when there is an issue deemed important by a sizable portion of the electorate on which, for one reason or another, neither of the major parties is responsive. The 1892 platform of the Prohibition party exemplifies the spirit of the single-purpose party.

> We arraign the Republican and Democratic Parties as false to the standards reared by their founders; as faithless to the principles of the illustrious leaders of the past to whom they do homage with the lips. . . . The competition of both the parties for the vote of the slums, and their assiduous courting of the liquor power and subserviency to the money power, has resulted in placing those powers in the position of practical arbiters of the

destinies of the nation. We renew our protest against these perilous tendencies, and invite all citizens to join us in the upbuilding of a party . . . that prefers temporary defeat to an abandonment of the claims of justice, sobriety, personal rights and the protection of American homes.

Recognizing and declaring that prohibition of the liquor traffic has become the dominant issue in national politics, we invite to full party fellowship all those who on this one dominant issue are with us agreed, in the full belief that this party can and will remove sectional differences, promote national unity, and insure the best welfare of our entire land.[4]

A third type of minor party is the sectional party, such as the Farmer-Labor party in Minnesota or the American Labor party in New York. Finally, there are the socioeconomic parties, such as the Socialist party.

Typically, a minor party is founded when a group of discontented political leaders are disturbed by the actions of one or both of the major parties. These leaders will argue that the major parties are unresponsive to the pressing needs of a substantial proportion of the electorate and that a new party is therefore needed. From the point of view of individual voters, a third party offers a home at a time when they do not think that the major parties are accommodating their needs. From the point of view of the functioning of the system, the fact that a new party may arise at any time helps keep the system responsive. It makes it unlikely that the two major parties will engage in a prolonged duopolistic agreement, tacit or explicit, or ignore a set of wants shared by a significant number of consumers. If the major parties should ignore these wants, a new, responsive party can arise.

The importance of minor parties to the political system is not adequately reflected in the amount of voter support they attract. In the House of Representatives and the Senate the major parties have been dominant ever since the Republican party emerged as a major party. Every presidential election since 1860 has been won by a candidate of one of the two major parties. In the average presidential election minor parties receive only about 5 percent of the vote.

[4]Kirk H. Porter, *National Party Platforms* (New York: Macmillan, 1924).

American history is nevertheless spotted with periods in which minor parties, for a time, played a role of importance: the Locofoco party following the Panic of 1837; the Liberty party in the 1840s and 1850s; the Know Nothing party, with its conviction that most of the ills that troubled the body politic could be traced to the immigration of undesirable types of persons; the Free Soil party, with its slogan "Free Soil, Free Speech, Free Labor and Free Man"; in the 1880s and 1890s there was the Greenback party, the Prohibition party, and the Populist party. In 1948 there was the Dixiecrat party and the Progressive party with Henry A. Wallace as its titular head.

In American history only one minor party, the Republican party, has managed to make the grade and become established as a major party. The advent of the Republican party did not mean the birth of a multiparty system. The Republican party simply became the second party as the Whigs, unable to unite on the issue of slavery, disappeared. Other parties have had a less illustrious history. The Anti-Masonic party was absorbed by the Whigs. The Locofocos were drawn into the Democratic party. The Know-Nothings were absorbed into the Republican party, as were the Free Soil party and the Liberty party.

In view of the record of minor parties, why do political leaders persist in third party efforts? The answer is not to be found in wholly rational political considerations. The drive behind a given third party effort may be found in a calculated attempt to force the hand of a major party or in a strong sense of outrage and protest. A leader's calculations concerning the prospects of such a movement may reflect a sober assessment of political realities or may be a product of little more than his hopes and personal ambitions. It is apparently easy for a third party leader to become a believer in the "doctrine of the hidden majority."[5] This doctrine tells its adherents that there are many persons who are eager to become politically active but who remain inactive, and even to a degree apolitical, because neither of the major parties will give them what they want. If a new party were to come along, or a new type of leader, or a leader espousing the things that this

[5] See Philip E. Converse, Aage A. Clausen, Warren Miller, "Electoral Myth and Reality: The 1964 Election," *American Political Science Review* (June, 1965), pp. 321–336.

hidden majority really favors, vast political energies could presumably be tapped. The doctrine of the hidden majority was apparently persuasive to George Wallace.[6]

It is important to understand why the number of major parties in the national market does not go below two and it is also important to understand why it does not go *above* two. Mechanical features of the system, such as election by plurality and single-member districts, go a long way to explain this. Another important factor, however, is the difficulty that third parties have in entering the market.[7]

The obstacles in the way of starting a new party to compete on even terms with the established parties are analogous to those in the way of starting a new automobile company to compete with the Big Three. There are problems of cost, and of fund raising; of attracting experienced personnel to a new organization and of keeping them despite party defeats; of developing a product that will be attractive to consumers yet sufficiently differentiated from those already available; of establishing regional and local marketing outlets and service organizations. In addition there is the problem of developing a satisfactory "name" in a market that is attuned to the established brand names, "Democratic party," "Republican party." Party identification, a potent electoral factor in the United States, favors the established parties.

A further difficulty is that the fledgling party, in asking for support, is not in a position to offer very much in return for that support. It is not able to promise the modification of public policy because it has little chance of winning office. Few voters will persist long in supporting a new party if the prospects of that party remain dim. A handful of voters might, of course; individual behavior in a political marketplace may be motivated by the desire to punish, to retaliate, and to deprive as well as by the more customary political values. Such motivations would provide an unstable basis for a political party, however, and are not ones on which a mass party could long be nourished. The difficulty in

---

[6]The attractions of the doctrine are not confined to third party leaders of course. Converse, Clausen, and Miller, ibid., discuss the doctrine in connection with the 1964 campaign of Senator Goldwater.

[7]See Gordon Tullock, "Entry Barriers in Politics," *American Economic Review*, LV (May, 1965), pp. 458–466.

starting a third party affords some protection to the major parties since it means that a major third party effort will not be undertaken casually. The harder it is to get a third party started under the conditions prevailing in the national market the greater is the latitude that the major parties have before this corrective process will start to work.

One of the most severe obstacles that a third party faces lies in the ability of the major parties to steal elements of its platform. A third party is most likely to arise when needs and attitudes have developed in the market to which neither of the major parties is responsive. The rise of a third party, however, is likely to make the major parties acutely aware of those needs and attitudes. Once the leaders of the major parties are aware they are likely to take positions which will cut the ground from beneath the fledgling third party. As soon as it became evident during the campaign of 1968 that George Wallace's emphasis on "law and order" was attractive to a great many Americans, the candidates of the major parties quickly adopted the issue. By election day there were three candidates who were calling sternly for law and order.

If a single issue provides the *raison d'être* of the third party, the very existence of the party becomes problematic once one of the major parties has taken a favorable position on the issue. The destiny of a third party, therefore, rests less in the hands of its own leadership than in the hands of the leaders of the major parties. Once the voters are given a choice between a major party that has taken a moderately attractive stand on an issue and a minor party that has taken an exceedingly attractive stand, they will gravitate toward the major party in the interest of political efficacy. When there is a strong demand for a political product, it will be bought from any organization that offers it, including a new and untried organization. Once a major party offers a product to meet that same demand, consumers will abandon the new organization in favor of the established one. It is noteworthy that despite the publicity the Wallace party received during the 1968 campaign and the broad support it seemed to have for a time, it polled only 13.4 percent of the total vote on election day and seemed to disappear from sight after the election.

A minor party may also be at a disadvantage because of the small size of the market for which it has potential appeal. Unless there is massive discontent with both of the major parties, the market for the products of a minor party will be small. Discontent with the party in power is more likely to express itself in terms of support for the opposition party than support for a third one. A minor party may pick up support quickly when it comes into being—and very quickly exhaust the market of voters who are already disenchanted with the major parties. Drawing large numbers of voters *away* from the established parties will prove more difficult.

One of the reasons it will prove difficult is that the minor party is apt to be severely handicapped by its lack of product diversification. If the insensitivity of the major parties to a new issue or need is the source of their vulnerability, the concentration of a minor party upon that issue or need is the source of *its* vulnerability. If a minor party is brought into being because of discontent with a stand of the major parties, its appeal will necessarily be limited to those consumers to whom that issue is of great importance. It is a characteristic of major parties, on the other hand, that they offer a wide variety of political products rather than a single product. The stand of the minor party may allow it to get a foothold in the market but its single-mindedness will prevent it from having a broad appeal. It has little to offer voters who are indifferent to that single issue.

If it tries to widen its appeal in order to attract more voters it may run the risk of a party split. Many of the members attracted to the party in the first instance were drawn to it because of its stand on a central issue and there is no assurance that these members will be in agreement on quite different issues. Furthermore the ideologues, whom a third party may attract in considerable number, may prefer doctrinal purity and single-mindedness of purpose rather than product diversification in the interest of a broader appeal. The party, therefore, may be trapped: if it does not broaden its appeal it cannot challenge the major parties; if it broadens its appeal it is likely to split and lose many of its more passionate members.

Some minor parties aspire to become major parties and when

they fail to achieve a breakthrough drop out of sight. Other minor parties persist and are to be found on the ballot in successive elections. The Socialist party, for example, seemed to be relatively stable at a low level of activity and support. It offered highly differentiated products having little mass appeal in the United States. Its products did appeal to a small and faithful clientele, however, and this support allowed it to stay in business.

Because it is so difficult to start a third party, those who are discontented often gravitate toward the expedient of a splinter party or toward efforts to capture the machinery, nationally or regionally, of one of the major parties. In a political market there is no law to prevent a brand name from being used by unauthorized persons. Any candidate for office can call himself a Democrat or a Republican. If he succeeds in getting himself officially nominated he *is* the official candidate of that party regardless of the extent to which his views may diverge from those of the national leadership. The ability of an individual to seek, and possibly win, nomination in a direct primary has probably reduced the pressure for the formation of third parties below what it otherwise would have been.

## Interest Organizations

It is a characteristic of large political markets that much of the significant communication within them is among organizations. There are major parties, minor parties, and scores of interest organizations. The three categories might be distinguished in the following way:

| | |
|---|---|
| **A major party** | 1) makes appeals to the entire electorate or major portions of it; |
| | 2) offers presidential candidates and candidates in a great many lesser markets across the nation. |
| **A minor party** | 1) makes appeals to the electorate that are somewhat restricted as to content or geographic scope; |
| | 2) may or may not offer a candidate for the presidency, but is not able to offer candidates in lesser markets across the nation. |

**An interest**  1) may make appeals to the electorate that
**organization**  are broad or restricted in content and geo-
graphic scope;
2) does not offer candidates for office.

Nonparty organizations vary greatly in size of membership, intensity of membership activity, geographical scope, effectiveness, objectives, techniques used in the pursuit of these objectives, and ideology. Because these organizations may be examined from so many points of view, there is no single basis for classification that is wholly satisfactory.

American history in the nineteenth and twentieth centuries has been influenced to no small extent by various of these organization—the Knights of Labor, the Grange, the Ku Klux Klan, the Anti-saloon League, the American Federation of Labor, the CIO (Congress of Industrial Organizations), CORE (Congress on Racial Equality), Southern Christian Leadership Conference, SNCC (Student Nonviolent Coordinating Committee), and on and on.

These organizations serve a variety of functions in the political marketplace. They are a part of the communication and opinion-making network that links major political producers, such as the parties, to the consumer. Their communications role is by no means wholly passive. They shape and color information and opinion as they transmit it and they influence both consumers and producers. Their role, in this respect, is somewhat analogous to that of communications media such as radio, press, and television, since they help to fill the void between consumers and producers.

Unlike the mass media, these organizations may also perform a brokerage function. Individual consumers register their market preferences in a variety of ways, and that includes joining interest organizations. These organizations are then in a position to represent the interests of their members in dealing with other organizations in the market. Interest groups stand between individuals, on the one hand, and political parties and governmental organizations on the other. They press the demands of their membership and, in so doing, often engage in bargaining on behalf of their members. It is a form of collective bargaining.

Bargaining presumes an exchange process, and the spokesmen for the organization are engaged in both buying and selling. They are seeking to sell the organization's program, its demands, its point of view, and the importance of its support to the parties and to governmental institutions. At the same time, in return for concessions to it, the organization may be asked to "buy" the candidates or program of a party, to support that party or to cease opposing it.

A broker, by definition, is a middleman. If the leadership of the organization has a series of relationships with political and governmental organizations, it also has relationships with its own membership. Its task will often be that of adjusting the demands and wants of its membership to the realities of the larger market situation. If the organization's leadership has extracted certain concessions from governmental leaders in return for various concessions on the part of the group, the leadership must then turn around and sell the terms of agreement to the rank-and-file membership.[8]

The position of the organization's leadership in such a situation is closely analogous to that of a union's leadership seeking to adjust the demands of the union members and the concessions proposed by management. The leaders of a union may be thought of as buying certain demands from the union membership and trying to sell those demands to management. Then it buys certain counterdemands from management and seeks to sell these to its membership as the necessary price for the desired concessions.

In the same way, the leaders of an interest organization buy certain things from their members and try to sell them to political and governmental organizations (figure below).

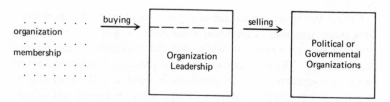

----

[8]Curry and Wade refer to these brokers as "fiduciaries." "The fiduciary is a political actor who represents beneficiaries as a group agent. His role within the system is to bargain with other group fiduciaries on issues in which his

Then the leaders must try to sell to the membership the concessions that it has bought from the political or governmental organizations (figure below).

Bargaining will often be complex and protracted, with each of the three actors buying and selling (figure below).

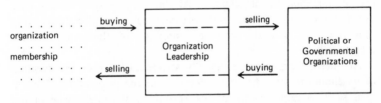

The terms agreed upon, at a given time, will be strongly influenced by the supply and demand situation in the market and by the relative market strengths of the participants in the negotiation. The interest group leaders may present initial demands, on behalf of their members, that will be deemed unreasonable. These demands, if acceded to, might require, say, a 40 percent increase in the operating budget of a federal agency. When the agency points out to the interest group leadership the implications of their demands, and maintains that the figure is unacceptable, the interest leadership may modify its position. Ultimately the agency might be prepared to go to Congress with requests for a 10 percent increase in funds to finance increased agency functions. In a somewhat similar way, the leaders of a major party might point out to the leaders of an interest organization that agreement with their demands would force a reshaping of the party's program and, furthermore, would alienate other groups supporting

beneficiaries have an interest and to compete with other group fiduciaries to affect the authoritative allocation of resources by the government on issues interesting to his beneficiaries." R. L. Curry and L. L. Wade, *A Theory of Political Exchange* (Englewood Cliffs, N. J.: Prentice-Hall, 1968), p. 41.

the party. They would argue, that is, that the costs of compliance with the group's demands would be prohibitive. The interest group's leadership in such circumstances, would go away empty-handed or with only minor concessions.

This discussion has emphasized the broker or middleman role of interest group leaders. It should be noted, however, that a broker may develop goals that are different from those of the individuals he is supposed to be representing and not wholly compatible. Whenever a degree of autonomy and independence *can* develop an observer should be alert to the prospect that it *will* develop. It should not be assumed that the leaders of an organization automatically seek the interests of the members of the organization in all respects. At the very least, a leader may develop a concern for personal prestige, salary, and style of living that may be at odds with the interests of the organization's members.[9]

An interest organization usually strives to improve the position of its clients relative to other elements in the population. Typically it seeks a larger share of the resources at the disposal of the political and economic system. In a complex modern democratic society such as the United States there will be a great many organizations and interests jousting for position and making simultaneous demands upon the political and economic system. Many of these demands will meet with disappointment: first, because the resources available are limited; second, because the demands may be mutually incompatible. If the demands of one group are satisfied it may be only at the price of disappointing the demands of another group. There is no natural harmony of interests.

When a new interest organization moves into the political arena it will not find itself in harmony with all existing organizations. For this reason there will be varying responses to its appearance, ranging from strong opposition to strong support, with many shades in between, including indifference. When the demands of groups are complementary, they may be able to engage in collaborative activity in the marketplace. If the demands are incompatible, so that the interests of one organization can only be advanced at the expense of the interests of another organization, the

[9]For an interesting discussion of related issues see Mancur Olson, Jr., *The Logic of Collective Action* (Cambridge: Harvard University Press, 1965).

groups are likely to engage in competitive activity. The effectiveness of an organization will be greatly influenced by the nature of the environmental response that it encounters. Since the environment is always in a process of change, the compatibility of an organization with its environment can vary widely over a period of time.

In addition to responding to changes in its environment, an interest organization may play an active role in changing that environment. It may educate consumers about the desirability of certain kinds of political products and may help generate political demands that other organizations, including parties, will have to satisfy. Interest groups are therefore a force for programmatic and ideological innovation. Without the formulation and propagation of ideas by interest organizations the American political system would lose a good deal of its adaptability and capacity for innovation.

The success of an interest organization will normally be related to its internal processes and to the demand and supply situation that it encounters in the market. The demand for an organization's product will depend largely on the extent to which the perceived ideology, objectives, behavior, and personnel of the organization are congruent with those found in the environment. An organization enjoying a high degree of congruence can normally expect to find a larger market for its products than an organization with low congruence.

Certain exceptions need to be pointed out, however. If the degree of congruence is so high that the products of the organization cannot be differentiated from those of other organizations, demand may be weak. If congruence is low, an organization may be able to survive, and even to thrive, by uncovering a special market that no other organization is catering to. The ideology and activities of the Ku Klux Klan, for example, have little congruence with the broad characteristics of the American political environment yet the Klan goes on year after year because it has found a restricted market in which its products are in great demand and in which it encounters little competition. An organization may be able to design its products with a particular subculture, minority, interest, or profession in mind and its acceptance in that market is closely connected to its lack of congruence with the society as a whole. There are a great many special political markets in the United States and many political organizations have come into being to meet the needs of those markets.

An interest organization usually strives for growth because the larger the number of consumers of its products, the more support it has in the market and the more effective it will be in dealing with other organizations and governmental agencies. The same logic encourages interest groups to ally with one another or even to amalgamate. Interest organizations do not invariably strive for this kind of expansion, however. An organization might be willing to sacrifice growth in favor of homogeneity and ideological cohesiveness. The National Association of Manufacturers, for example, is apparently content to operate on the basis of a small number of supporting firms since this allows it to achieve a high level of doctrinal consensus. The NAM can usually take stronger stands on issues than can a more broadly based organization such as the United States Chamber of Commerce.

How an interest organization or a political party uses its support and influence will depend on its general position in the market and on a number of considerations of strategy—matters to be examined in the following chapter.

# Chapter Four
# Markets and Marketing

## Communications and the Market Process

The functioning of the American political system cannot be described or understood adequately except with reference to communications. This is true of the system as a whole and it also holds for a number of the subprocesses within that system, such as the electoral process. As the capacity to trace and analyze the flow of communications increases, understanding of the political process will also improve.

No large market can function without a communications system. In the absence of signals flowing through that communications system, buyers cannot know what is being offered nor the cost of available products and sellers cannot know what is being demanded. Exchange itself cannot be carried on in the absence of negotiation and communication among potential buyers and potential sellers. When it is recalled that the political system of the United States involves an intricate complex of linked markets, the importance of communication becomes obvious.

It is also obvious that the combined information requirements of this complex of markets and submarkets is staggering. To service this complex there exists a vast communications network of transmitters, receivers, relay stations, filters—the array of elements found in any sophisticated communications system. Signals

43

move through this network to be stored, to be ignored, or to serve as cues for a variety of actions, reactions, and adjustments. The flow of communications through this network is little understood as yet, but messages can be observed moving from one market to another, from one party to another, from one element in a party to another, from parties to private organizations and the reverse, from one government to another, from governmental units to private organizations, from one leader to another. These messages also move by means of a variety of different channels—telephone, the mails, newspapers, magazines, radio, television, and face-to-face communication.

The communications system has a great deal of flexibility in the way that it handles political information. It normally operates at a fraction of its potential capacity. During political campaigns and the period prior to the nomination of candidates, however, the flow of communications picks up sharply. Channels of communication that are seldom used for political purposes may be activated for a time before returning to a stage of dormancy. Since different channels are used to reach audiences in the various markets, the kinds of messages that flow through the different channels will vary. There may also be a noticeable variation in the kinds of messages that flow through a single channel at different times. The amount of distortion associated with communications will vary with the channel, the user, and the nature of the communication.

Because the communications system and the political system are so closely linked, changes in the former necessarily affect the latter. For example, the advent of television has altered to some extent the qualities that voters consider important in candidates and hence has had an impact upon the kind of candidates that parties are inclined to nominate. If a candidate is not reasonably attractive, does not have a relaxed television manner, and does not project an image of competence and sincerity, his chances of being nominated and elected are reduced. Television has revolutionized campaigning. A number of observers have argued, for instance, that the televised debates between John F. Kennedy and Richard Nixon were a turning point in the 1960 campaign. Television coverage of national conventions has had an impact upon the conduct of those conventions. The use by the television networks on election day of computer-aided predictions of election outcomes may have an impact on voting in western states where polling places do not close until some hours after they close in the east.

The mass media serve as important communications links between the producers of political products and the consumers of such products. Messages flow in both directions through the media. Consumers learn about the products being offered and producers are enabled to guage consumer preferences and responses. Since the mass media are much more than simple transmitters of messages they can and do influence the political process in a variety of significant ways.

The influence of the communications system as a whole upon the political system is substantial and is more or less continuous, but there is also a reciprocal influence. Politics has an impact upon communications as well. For one thing, it commands a great deal of attention from the media. For another, political processes may be used to regulate the behavior of the media and to shape the development of the communications system in general. The federal government licenses television and radio stations, supervises competition in the communications industry, requires equal time for candidates on television, and so forth.

## Consumption: Individual Choice and Collective Decision-Making

Political participation usually involves the consumption of political products. When a voter votes for a candidate he is "buying" that candidate, at least to the extent of voting for him. When he writes his congressman in favor of a proposed antismog bill he is accepting the bill. When he writes a check to the Republican National Committee he is buying the products offered by the Republican party. The rich literature on political participation is, therefore, at the same time, a literature on the consumption of political products.[1] The material available on voting behavior

[1]If "political participation" and "consumption" are such closely related terms, what is the advantage in using a new and unfamiliar term? The answer is that the term "political participation" does not suggest links with other elements in the political system. The term "consumption," on the other hand, keeps the analyst aware of the relationship of the behavior being observed to other types of behavior characterized by the terms production, distribution, marketing, exchange.

throws a great deal of light on the behavior of individuals and groups of individuals in a political market—the impact of attitudes, personality, beliefs, personal contact, particular issues, social position, age, sex, religion, opinion leaders, and membership in subgroups and subcultures.[2]

Party identification, for example, is an important factor in voting. Eight of ten persons will normally vote in accordance with party identification. The individual who votes for the party he identifies with finds his task much eased. He does not need to invest effort in learning about candidates because, in the last analysis, all he needs to know about them is their party label. He does not need to study the issues involved in an election because they are irrelevant to the basis on which he will make his decision.

What of the individual who does more than just vote and who participates actively in the political process? He, too, is engaging in an exchange process. He pays certain costs (time expended, alternative income not earned, and so on) in return for various gains (heightened sense of belonging and group identification, increased status and prestige in the eyes of others, gratification of sense of duty, material benefits such as a larger number of clients for his law office).[3] The extent of an individual's political participation will be influenced by his projection of probable costs and benefits. If he expects that the benefits from further participation will increase more rapidly than the costs of such participation he is likely to become more active. This line of thought, when applied not merely to a single individual but collectively, suggests that the more intensive forms of political participation can be analyzed helpfully in terms of demand and supply. If the benefits from participation increase, this can be interpreted as an increase in the "demand" for participation. Increased numbers of individuals will presumably be drawn into political participation as a

[2]There is a rich literature on political participation. See for example Angus Campbell, Philip E. Converse, Warren E. Miller, and Donald E. Stokes, *The American Voter* (New York: Wiley, 1960). Lester W. Milbrath's more recent study, *Political Participation* (Chicago: Rand McNally, 1965) is also very helpful. This book incorporates an excellent bibliography.

[3]For an analysis of the motivation of political participants see Robert E. Lane, *Political Life: Why People Get Involved in Politics* (Glencoe, Ill.: Free Press, 1959).

consequence of the increased payoff. If the benefits from participation drop, the level of participation should drop also (assuming that the costs are unchanged).

Two distinct, but closely related, questions need to be touched on. The first has to do with the nature of individual choice and its rationality or lack of it; the second with the relation of individual choice to collective decision-making. There is a distinct difference between the way political scientists have approached the matter of individual choice and the way economists have approached it. Political scientists have not sought to develop a "theory" of individual choice but have gathered data on the attitudes and decisions of individuals. Economic choice theory on the other hand is far more rigorous than its political science counterpart but is unabashedly deductive. It begins with a set of assumptions and moves carefully to assorted conclusions. Because it is rigorous and highly general, the economic theory of choice has relevance to noneconomic variables.[4] It examines the question of goal attainment within the context of limited resources. This requires the allocation of resources among competing uses and the use of a ranking system as a starting point. In this scheme the individual is assumed to have goals or purposes, to have the capacity to pursue those goals (that is, rationality), and to do this by trying to maximize his "utility." The assumptions underlying this model have not been adequately justified on theoretical grounds because utility theory assumes that satisfactions can be measured cardinally and added to one another. Nevertheless the theory has been a useful one.

For many purposes utility theory has been replaced by indifference analysis, which does not require the assumption made by utility analysis. The individual does not try to maximize utility but, instead, seeks to move to a preferred position.

> The result of abandoning, for the most part, the idea that satisfactions can be added means that indifference curve analysis of the behavior of a rational individual has taken the place of the Marshallian type of analysis. The assumption that the individual

[4]See Eugene V. Schneider and Sherman Krupp, "An Illustration of the Use of Analytical Theory in Sociology: The Application of the Economic Theory of Choice to Non-Economic Variables," *The American Journal of Sociology*, LXX (May, 1965), pp. 695–703.

tries to maximize his satisfaction is retained, although to maximize satisfaction no longer means achieving the largest sum total of satisfaction, but rather reaching the most preferred possible position. An individual can say that he is higher up on a hill, or lower down a hill, or at the same height, but, unlike ordinary numbers, such estimates are not marked in feet, or units of satisfaction.[5]

Indifference analysis centers on the concept of Pareto optimality.

The criterion that the modern welfare economist employs in determining whether or not a given situation is "efficient" or "optimal" and whether or not a given move or change is "efficient" or "optimal" was developed by Vilfredo Pareto. . . .

The underlying premise of the modern Paretian construction is the purely individualistic one. The individual himself is assumed to be the only one who is able to measure or to quantify his own utility or satisfaction. No external observer is presumed able to make comparisons of utility among separate individuals. It is possible, however, even within these limits, to develop a means of evaluating either "situations" or "change in situations" in terms of their "efficiency." To do this, a very weak ethical postulate is advanced. The "welfare" of the whole group of individuals is said to be increased if (1) every individual in the group is made better off, or (2) if at least one member in the group is made better off without anyone being made worse off. . . . The ambiguities in the terms "better off" and "worse off" are removed by equating these to the individual's own preferences. If an individual shifts to position A from position B when he could have freely remained in B, he is presumed to be "better off" at B than at A.[6]

Utility analysis and indifference analysis both make assumptions regarding the rationality of individual behavior.[7] One of the

[5]R. L. Curry and L. L. Wade, *A Theory of Political Exchange: Economic Reasoning in Political Analysis* (Englewood Cliffs, N. J.: Prentice-Hall), p. 31. The discussion in this volume of utility theory and indifference analysis is a useful one.

[6]James Buchanan and Gordon Tullock, *The Calculus of Consent: Logical Foundations of Constitutional Democracy* (Ann Arbor: University of Michigan Press, 1962), pp. 171–172. Pareto optimality is also discussed helpfully in James M. Buchanan, "Positive Economics, Welfare Economics, and Political Economy," *Journal of Law and Economics*, II (1959).

[7]For an interesting treatment of some of the formal aspects of the rationality question see Kenneth J. Arrow, *Social Choice and Individual Values* (New York: Wiley, 1951).

most suggestive discussions of political rationality is that appearing in Anthony Downs' *An Economic Theory of Democracy.*[8] Downs has emphasized that the question of "rationality" must be examined in connection with anticipated costs and benefits to the individual involved. If an individual is to make informed political decisions he must gather information and analyze the probable outcomes of alternative lines of action. For those in some professions or walks of life it may be difficult to gather this information and may require a substantial investment of time. The acquisition of politically relevant information involves costs to the individual and he may wonder whether those costs are more than offset by attendant benefits. He might rationally conclude that it is not worth his while, in terms of costs and benefits, to try to become an informed voter. Casting a casual, careless vote may be thoroughly rational behavior in the circumstances.

The same sort of cost/benefit analysis might also incline an individual to abstain from political participation altogether. If he were persuaded that the man who casts a careless vote is acting irresponsibly, then he must either become well-informed or not vote at all. In such circumstances he might reasonably choose the latter. Political apathy need not always be viewed as a disease. Sometimes it should be seen as a rational response on the part of an individual to the conflict between the requirements for informed participation, on the one hand, and the direction of his personal interests, on the other. It is not reasonable to ask that everyone be interested in political affairs.

Lack of information is one of the most important obstacles to wise choice. An individual may not know what each party stands for, what individual candidates stand for, and what those parties and candidates will actually try to do if placed in office. He may not be able to distinguish the products of one party from those of another and may therefore be heavily influenced by the appearance, style, and public relations skills of the contestants. His capacity to make wise decisions will also be interfered with by illusion.

> Behavior under illusion is not necessarily irrational. The individual who behaves irrationally makes inconsistent choices; he does not behave in such a way that an external observer can make predictions, even should his utility function remain

[8] (New York: Harper & Row, 1957.)

unchanged. By contrast, the individual who behaves in the presence of an illusion will act consistently; given the same choice situation on two separate occasions he will tend to make the same decision, provided that "learning from experience" does not dispel the illusion and provided that his utility function does not shift in the interim. Conceptually, the external observer can make predictions here if he knows the effects of illusion on choice behavior. This amounts to saying that "theorizing" about individual behavior under illusion is possible, whereas "theorizing" about individual behavior that is genuinely irrational is not possible.[9]

The question of rationality is an intriguing one but is not central to a discussion of the market approach. Analysts who wish to proceed deductively can scarcely avoid making an assumption of rationality but political scientists, less committed to the deductive approach can sidestep the issue. They can observe that, as a practical matter, political markets have been functioning fairly well for a long time which means that certain minimums of collective rationality must have been satisfied.[10]

The second question to be discussed, as noted earlier, has to do with the relationship of individual choice to collective decision-making. The operation of the American political system involves the making of countless individual choices. When the individual makes a personal choice he is often participating in community choice as well. How does this process work? How are individual decisions translated into collective decisions?

Economists have been interested in the same question as it applies to economic markets. They have been able to use the individual calculus to explain the workings of many elements in the economic system.[11] Others use the individual calculus to ex-

[9]James Buchanan, *Public Finance in Democratic Process* (Chapel Hill: University of North Carolina Press, 1967), p. 127.

[10]"To be sure, many individual voters act in odd ways indeed; yet in the large the electorate behaves about as rationally and responsibly as we should expect, given the clarity of the alternatives presented to it and the character of the information available to it." V. O. Key, Jr., *The Responsible Electorate: Rationality in Presidential Voting* 1936–1940 (Cambridge: Harvard University Press, 1966), p. 7.

[11]The economics of collective choice as it relates to social goods is discussed in Howard Bowen's *Toward Social Economy* (New York: Holt, Rinehart and Winston, 1948).

plain significant elements of social behavior.[12] James Buchanan and Gordon Tullock have sought to make systematic use of the individual calculus in the analysis of politics.[13]

The means by which private choices are combined to produce collective political outcomes has not been adequately analyzed. What kind of cost/benefit calculations do individuals make? How do calculations of private benefits and costs relate to calculations about public benefits and costs?[14] How does the individual cope with the realization that what he wants in a political market may be quite different from what he gets? He rarely confronts a situation in which there is complete correspondence between his own preferences and the outcome of the collective process.[15] When a voter makes a decision to support a given program, how much thought does he give to the probable costs associated with that program if it is approved?

Much remains to be learned about individual choice and the way in which political markets convert such choices into collective decisions. One of the most intriguing features of the process is the capacity of the market to generate collective decisions that are accepted as legitimate. The market process does not reconcile conflicting wants in the sense that everyone emerges favoring the

[12]See, for example, John W. Thibaut and Harold H. Kelley, *The Social Psychology of Groups* (New York: Wiley, 1959); and Peter M. Blau, *Exchange and Power in Social Life* (New York: Wiley, 1964).

[13]"Can the pursuit of individual self-interest be turned to good account in politics as well as in economics? We have tried to outline the sort of calculus that the individual must undergo when he considers this question. We have discussed the formation of organizational rules that might result from such a rational calculus. In our more rigorous analytical models we have adopted the extreme assumption that each participant in the political process tries, single-mindedly, to further his own interest, at the expense of others if this is necessary. We were able to show that, even under such an extreme behavioral assumption, something closely akin to constitutional democracy as we know it would tend to emerge from rational individual calculus. We believe that this in itself is an important proof that should assist in the construction of a genuine theory of constitutional democracy." *The Calculus of Consent: Logical Foundations of Constitutional Democracy* (Ann Arbor: University of Michigan Press, 1962), pp. 304–305.

[14]See the excellent article by James S. Coleman, "Foundations for a Theory of Collective Decisions," *The American Journal of Sociology*, LXXI, No. 6 (May, 1966).

[15]See James Buchanan's *Fiscal Theory and Political Economy* (Chapel Hill: University of North Carolina Press, 1960), Chapter IV.

same policies. Instead it produces decisions that are accepted as legitimate because of the way that they are made. In 1968 almost as many voters supported Hubert Humphrey as Richard Nixon. Sixty-nine million votes were cast and Nixon's margin was only slightly over 300,000. Yet there was never any doubt that the massive minority who voted for Humphrey would accept the outcome. In the 1960 election when Richard Nixon lost by an even smaller margin no disgruntled mobs took to the streets.

To say that the decisions that emerge from this process are widely accepted is not to say that they are the best possible decisions. Individuals do not have the same wants and they do not have the same priorities among their wants. No mechanism can guarantee that collective decision-making will produce optimal outcomes. The market process transmutes individual decisions into collective decisions but there is no guarantee that those decisions will always be wise or fair. The market process will not always respond to the full range of needs in the society and it may well produce outcomes that are more to the advantage of one group than another.

## Markets and Marketing

Major parties, minor parties, and interest organizations all seek to market their products. The history of these organizations can be analyzed in terms of their success in producing and marketing products that are attractive to consumers. By the same token, the history of particular products can be analyzed in terms of their reception in the market. Each product has something akin to a life cycle. If the product is an individual, he may come on the scene as an interesting and exciting new face—a young Harold Stassen or "Soapy" Williams riding out of the west. After time, and a few campaigns, his is no longer a new face, and his marketability may drop sharply. Even popular generals and national heroes can become tiresome after a while.

Issues may be regarded as political products and they, too, have life cycles which may vary greatly. A concern with news management or with vicuna coats in high places may last four months. A concern with "Communists in government" may last four years and a concern with slavery last four decades. There is perpetual change among issues in the marketplace. New ones continue to arise, with better or worse prospects for longevity, and old ones fade and die. A cluster of socioeconomic issues emerged during the Progressive Era, reached maturity during the New Deal period, hung on with declining importance through the 1940s, and faded rapidly after that. Soviet-American relations have been an issue since the end of World War II although the nature of the issue is changing. In one sense, the role of the Negro in American life has been an issue for 150 years. In another sense, however, a cluster of new issues pertaining to the Negro and American life have arisen since the early 1950s.

Parties and interest groups offer their products in the political markets of the nation. Some of these markets are defined by a set of geographical boundaries—ward, precinct, school district, nation, legislative district, congressional district, and state. Other markets cut across geographical boundaries–the young, the elderly, the Jewish community, the Negroes, the poor, the business community, and the like. All of these markets have certain features in common and each of them has special characteristics.

Each of these markets exists in an environment that includes a variety of other markets, and each market will be related to the others to some extent. They may be linked vertically. For example, events in a state market will be heavily influenced by events in the cities of that state. What happens in a city will be influenced by what happens in individual wards and precincts. Markets may also be linked horizontally; what happens in the eastern part of the state may be greatly influenced by what happens in the western part.

Unless a market is unusually isolated, events in it cannot be fully understood without reference to what is happening in the markets with which it is linked. If a presidential campaign is under way, for example, thousands of smaller markets are affected. Outputs from the national market serve as inputs into the smaller markets. During off-year elections, on the other hand, the input from the national market into a legislative district may be slight, while the input from the state-wide market, in which a gubernatorial race is taking place, may be great. The flow of inputs and outputs among markets can be quite complex. Market *A* may influence market *B*, which influences *C*, which influences *D*. Yet *A*'s influence may be only one of a number of influences that act on *D*. As the analytic tools of political science improve, it may be possible to trace these flows with some accuracy and to acquire an improved understanding of the political system in consequence.

## Marketing and Political Strategy

Marketing involves the advertising, distribution, and sale of political products. It provides a link by which producers and consumers are joined. The importance of effective marketing to a political party is obvious but what effective marketing dictates at any given moment is less so. Marketing involves considerations of strategy. Indeed it might be helpful for party leaders to think of parties as engaged in a game of strategy. The ingredients for such a game are all present:

- several participants
- sharing a mixture of common and conflicting interests
- competing in an environment having certain characteristics
- behavior governed by certain rules of the game
- with the actions of each party having an influence upon the behavior of the other.

Considerations of strategic interaction ought to influence many decisions relating to marketing. Should effort be directed toward creating a favorable image of the party itself or toward selling a particular program or candidate? Should attention be concentrated on trying to attract the undecided or on holding the following that the party already has? Should party leaders seek to maximize gains for their party or to do maximum harm to the opposition party? How aggressive and ruthless should a party be? Is cutthroat activity counterproductive in a stable market? Under what circumstances, if any, would it pay off? Since parties have common interests as well as conflicting interests, what types of collaboration between the two parties should be fostered? Under what circumstances should a party concentrate on building a basis for long-term electoral superiority rather than pursue a strategy aimed at immediate victory? Or, stating the question another way, how is the strategy for a single-play game related to the strategy for a repeated-play game?

An important aspect of political strategy is alliance-making. With what elements in a party or in society as a whole should a political leader seek to form an alliance?[16] If his strength is increased by the strength of his allies, why does he not pursue a policy of wholesale alliance? The answer is, of course, that the formation of an alliance is costly. A political group might offer its support—in return for an agreement to do or not to do certain things. The price to be paid for this support may rule out a broad system of alliances. That is, $A$'s agreement with $B$ may rule out an agreement with $C$. $B$ and $C$ may not be able to work together, or actor $A$ may have made a concession to $B$ that is unacceptable to $C$. When $A$ calculates the cost of his alliance with $B$, he must include in his calculations the loss of the support of $C$.

The leaders of each party will have to give some thought to the organizations that the party wants to work through and with. Many of the individual consumers that a party will want to influence can be most easily reached through the organizations with which they are associated—church, business organizations, civic associations, clubs. If individuals are thought of as ultimate consumers of a party's products, a two-stage distribution process is necessary, with the products going first to an organization and then to the organization's membership. In practice, however, it may be more helpful to think of the organization itself as a consumer. Marketing efforts are then aimed at an organization and its leadership, and what happens after that is not the direct concern of the party. Some candidates even carry this approach so far that they will strenuously seek to get the endorsement of an organization with little concern for the extent to which the endorsement either represents organization policy or will actually influence the voting behavior of rank-and-file members.

Party leaders may also wish to consider what use they can make of other instruments that lie at hand such as one or both houses of Congress, committees in the Congress, executive agencies, the judicial branch, or the state governments. Political use is frequently made of the institutions of government or the processes

[16]It is illuminating to examine both the internal and external affairs of parties in connection with the theory of alliances and coalitions. See William Riker, *The Theory of Political Coalition* (New Haven: Yale University Press, 1962).

of government. A president who directs the attorney general to proceed vigorously on civil rights matters is probably not unaware that this course may influence Negro voters at the next election. A president who has the opportunity to appoint several men to the Supreme Court will probably not be unaware that he can make appointments that will help change the image of the court, its policies, and its impact upon political attitudes in the country. Party leaders are usually conscious of the political impact that policy stands are likely to have.[17] They will need to consider not merely the impact of a particular stand but the impact of alternative policy mixes.

Party managers will want to adapt their strategy to the distribution of political attitudes in the marketplace. If the distribution is a normal one, neither party should move far from that part of the ideological spectrum where the greatest potential for political support is to be found. For example, if a conservative faction should gain control of a political party, party *A*, and move it well to the right along the Left/Right continuum, that party is likely to suffer at the polls. This situation is depicted in the figure below.

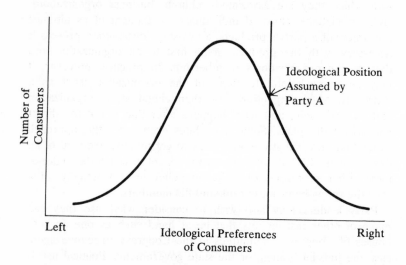

Ideological Position Assumed by Party A

Number of Consumers

Left

Ideological Preferences of Consumers

Right

[17]"Upon this reasoning rests the fundamental hypothesis of our model: parties formulate policies in order to win elections, rather than win elections in order to formulate policies." Anthony Downs, *An Economic Theory of Democracy* (New York: Harper & Row, 1957), p. 28.

In terms of pure strategy, the correct course for party *B* would be to assume a position slightly to the left of party *A*. This would allow party *B* to dominate those segments of the political spectrum in which the greatest distribution of voters are to be found. In practice, of course, party *B* might not find this an easy strategy to follow. The more ardent liberal leaders in party *B* might well feel betrayed by the thought of *B*'s taking a stand to the right of center and might argue that this would not give voters a real choice.

It is a commonplace that American political parties are seldom ideological. The explanation is not hard to find: It rarely pays to be ideological. Whether it will pay or not depends on the nature of the market at the moment. In 1932 and 1936, during a period of great change and adjustment, it paid the Democratic party to dramatize the new and distinctive elements in its ideology and program. During the period of domestic calm prior to the 1964 election, however, it did not pay Senator Goldwater to campaign on the basis of a restricted and sectarian appeal. At that time the two parties were operating on the basis of divergent estimates of the ideological preferences of consumers. The Democrats assumed a normal distribution of preferences, such as that indicated by the curve above. Senator Goldwater, on the other hand, apparently assumed a distribution of consumer preferences producing a curve skewed well to the right, as in the figure below. The election results showed that Senator Goldwater's perceptions were wide of the mark. If a party is to take full advantage of its strategic opportunities, it will need to be ideologically adaptable. If it becomes locked into a doctrinaire position it will be penalized at the polls.

Ideological and programmatic adaptation may take years or even decades. In 1952, after defeating Senator Robert A. Taft for the Republican presidential nomination, Dwight D. Eisenhower campaigned as a carrier of the ideas of a "New Republicanism." His victories in 1952 and 1956 did not mean that the Republican party had changed once and for all, however, as evidenced by the candidacy of Barry Goldwater in 1964. On the other hand, adaptation to the emergence of a new political technique may be much more rapid. During the campaign of 1956 Democratic party spokesmen complained that the use by the Republicans of public relations firms and "Madison Avenue techniques" was endangering the vital relationship between candidate and voter. By 1960, however, the Democratic party was making use of those techniques itself and its spokesmen no longer agonized about their long-run implications.

If political party $A$ is enjoying a competitive advantage because of a product it is offering or a technique it is using, this fact is not likely to be lost on party $B$. In an effort to share those high returns, party $B$ is likely to market a product quite similar to that offered by $A$. There are no patent laws governing political products, so $B$ is free to copy $A$ if it is able to do so. As a practical matter, of course, the product that $B$ offers will not be wholly identical to that offered by $A$ but will be presented as a new and improved version of $A$'s program or policy. If the product offered by party $A$ were in great demand and if *only* party $A$ could satisfy that demand, $A$'s competitive position would be very strong. It would be able to reap the political equivalent of monopoly profits.

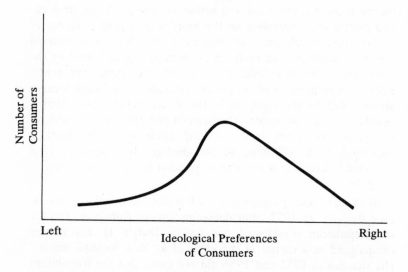

The major political parties are fairly responsive to changing market conditions but the analyst should be aware of the obstacles in the way of such responsiveness. They appear to take two forms. First, American parties have organizational characteristics which may impede response. They are large, decentralized, and they suffer from inertia. The second type of impediment has to do with the structure and characteristics of a given market. For example, if the attachment of voters to a party is unusually strong, the pressure on that party to adjust to changing demand is reduced. It may be able to offer obsolescent products for quite some time before substantial numbers of voters will begin to deny it support. If the products of the major parties are heavily differentiated, slight changes in the products produced by one may not lead to adjustments by the other. Broad product differentiation would mean that the two parties are perceiving the market in different ways and are not trying to follow one another's moves closely. If both parties were agreed on the nature of market demand, and were wrong, and if the obstacles to entry of a third party were great, the party system might be a long time in adjusting to market change.

Sometimes a party may respond segmentally to a changing market situation. Party leaders in one area may become aware of a problem and develop a way of responding to it long before the national party has taken cognizance of the problem. In a decentralized party system, such as is found in the United States, a local party might even disavow the national party in order to achieve local advantage. If local leaders believe that they can compete more effectively in the local market by disavowing or modifying the products of the national organization, they are free to do so. In this respect, local leaders or candidates are like wholesalers or distributors. They can give a discount to favored customers or cut the price on the products that they are marketing locally. This flexibility sometimes makes it possible for a candidate and local consumers to continue to give adherence to a party whose national positions they cannot accept. They simply ignore those positions. This is one of the reasons why the Democratic party in New York City can be so different from the Democratic party in, say, California or Mississippi.

Party strategy should take into account the size of a market. In the national market the marketing process is depersonalized. For the most part, producers and consumers do not meet face-to-face but via the mass media. A smaller market allows for a higher degree of personalization of politics. The candidate for town mayor or county commissioner can utilize a more intimate style of campaigning than can a presidential or even a gubernatorial candidate.

Party strategy should also be adapted to the structure of a market. A market that is highly organized would be treated differently from one that is only slightly organized. A state market that has a strong two-party system should be treated differently from one that has a weak two-party system or a one-party system.

After the outlines of the broad strategy have been decided upon, scores of subordinate decisions must be made. How can a party's products be packaged and distributed most effectively? Which promotional techniques or channels are likely to be most effective in a given market? Should new channels be developed? How great a marketing effort should be undertaken and how should that effort be scheduled?

The amount of a particular political product that is consumed within a given period of time is often closely related to the strenuousness with which the product is marketed. Other things being equal, the greater the marketing effort the larger the volume of sales. If the relationship between marketing effort and sales were constant, the result could be depicted by a straight line, $AA_1$

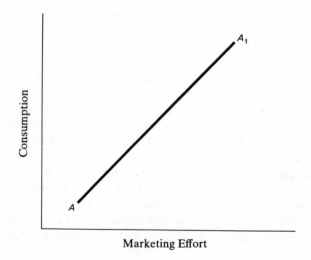

Marketing Effort

For most products, however, the relationship would not be linear. At some point, the yield from a given increment of additional effort would begin to fall. The relationship might be depicted by a curve, such as $BB_1$ or $CC_1$ or $DD_1$.

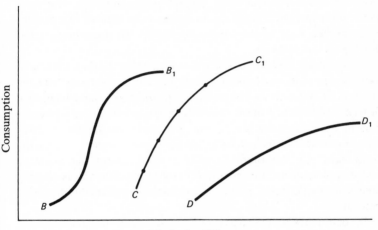

Marketing Effort

The precise character of the curve would vary from product to product since the consumer responses themselves vary.

If the consumption curves for individual products could be aggregated one would have a curve indicating the level of consumption in the market that would result from a given level of marketing effort. (To be sure, the shape and location of the curve would change as market conditions changed.) Such a curve might be useful in studying some of the problems associated with political apathy. The analyst would be able to estimate the level of marketing effort needed to call forth a given level of consumption at a given time.

## State and Municipal Markets

The problems faced by a state political organization may be very different from those faced by a national organization. If the state organization has the freedom to respond independently to those problems it is likely to do so. This means that developments in a particular market may be thoroughly out of step with developments on the national scene or in other markets. It is not unusual to find issues continuing to be fought in one market that have long since ceased to be controversial in other markets. For example, in most states the teaching of evolutionary doctrine ceased to be a point at issue several generations ago. Not until 1967, however, did Tennessee finally do away with its law prohibiting the teaching of evolution—the same law that precipitated the Scopes trial in 1925.

Competition may be more active in a state market than in a national one but, more often, is less so. The same holds true for other markets, such as congressional districts and state legislative districts. Historically there has been a low level of party alternation in a great many states, not just those in the South.[18] In those markets in which there is a high degree of party regularity, consumers buy the products of one party almost automatically and it is difficult for an opposition party to make headway. It may take a dramatic issue, event, or candidate to shake this behavior pattern.

In one market, interparty competition may be genuine and active, in another, little more than a formality. The disadvantaged party may, indeed, concede the market for all practical purposes, choosing not to allocate energies or resources to such an unlikely prospect. The absence of interparty competition does not necessarily imply the absence of all competition in a market, for there may be intraparty competition. Bifactional or multifactional competition may not serve the same political function as interparty competition, however.

> The legend prevails that within the Democratic Party in the southern states factional groups are the equivalent of political parties elsewhere. In fact, the Democratic Party in most states of the south is merely a holding company for a congeries of transient, squabbling factions, most of which fail by far to meet

[18]See Joseph A. Schlesinger, "A Two-dimensional Scheme for Classifying States According to Degree of Inter-party Competition," *The American Political Science Review*, vol. 49, pp. 1120–1129, December, 1955. This article looks at gubernatorial elections from 1870 to 1950 and finds a low rate of party alternation in nearly all states. More than half the states gave the governorship to one party in 70 percent or more of the elections.

the standards of permanence, cohesiveness, and responsibility that characterize the political party.[19]

There may be three, four, five, or even a half-dozen candidates seeking an office in a southern state, each bargaining with the others, each building and utilizing a temporary organization little related to previous organizations. In circumstances of this kind, "friends-and-neighbors voting" (that is, voting for the candidate from your part of the state) is often extremely important. The candidate is selling little more than his local or regional popularity. Consumers are not offered distinct political programs or tendencies and the result is a politics that is close to issue-free. More precisely, it is a politics of factionalism that is likely to mute all issues other than those revolving around personality and regional friction within the state.

The ability of the voters to punish the "ins" by withdrawing their support in favor of another party is central to the functioning of a two-party system. In a one-party market characterized by factionalism and the politics of personality, this option is not open to the voters. In most southern states, for example, one cannot punish the Democrats and reward the Republicans because there is no alternative to the Democratic party. All that voters can do to show their disapproval is to reject this individual or that passing coalition. This pattern is changing in some states, to be sure, and an observer can watch a one-party market being transformed into a two-party market.

The workings of traditional politics in a big city are easily analyzed in terms of the processes of exchange. An Italian may be included on the party slate to attract the Italian vote and a Pole to attract the Polish vote. A city machine may undertake to meet certain of the voters' needs in return for the support of those voters on election day. It would meet these needs by means of street paving, contracts, building permits, concessions, nonenforcement of ordinances, jobs, food, shelter, and so on. William L. Riordon's volume, *Plunkitt of Tammany Hall*, describes the process in some detail.

> What tells in holdin' your grip on your district is to go right down among the poor families and help them in the different

[19]V. O. Key, *Southern Politics* (New York: Knopf, 1949), p. 16.

ways they need help. I've got a regular system for this. If there's a fire in Ninth, Tenth, or Eleventh Avenue, for example, any hour of the day or night, I'm usually there with some of my election district captains as soon as the fire engines. If a family is burned out I don't ask whether they are Republicans or Democrats, and I don't refer them to the Charity Organization Society, which would investigate their case in a month or two and decide they were worthy of help about the time they are dead from starvation. I just get quarters for them, buy clothes for them if their clothes were burned up, and fix them up till they get things runnin' again. It's philanthropy, but its politics, too—mighty good politics. Who can tell how many votes one of these fires brings me? The poor are the most grateful people in the world, and, let me tell you, they have more friends in their neighborhoods than the rich have in theirs.[20]

Riordon includes a more concrete account.

2 A.M.:    Aroused from sleep by the ringing of his doorbell; went to the door and found a bartender, who asked him to go to the police station and bail out a saloon-keeper who had been arrested for violating the excise law. Furnished bail and returned to bed at three o'clock. . . .

8:30 A.M.:    Went to the police court to look after his constituents. Found six "drunks." Secured the discharge of four by a timely word with the judge, and paid the fines of two.

9 A.M.:    Appeared in the Municipal District Court. Directed one of his district captains to act as counsel for a widow against whom dispossess proceedings had been instituted and obtained an extension of time. Paid the rent of a poor family about to be dispossessed and gave them a dollar for food.

11 A.M.:    At home again. Found four men waiting for him. One had been discharged by the Metropolitan Railway Company for neglect of duty, and wanted the district leader to fix things. Another wanted a job on the road. The third sought a place on the Subway and the fourth, a plumber, was looking for work with the Consolidated Gas Company. The district leader spent nearly three hours fixing things for the four men, and succeeded in each case.[21]

[20]William L. Riordon, *Plunkitt of Tammany Hall* (New York: Knopf, 1948, originally published in 1905), pp. 36–37.
[21]Riordan, pp. 123–124.

The account continues until Plunkitt dropped into bed at midnight.

As long as a city machine controlled City Hall, no other organization could compete with it in its capacity to render services, do favors, and coerce enemies. The organization provided services all year long and on election day the debts were paid and the organization received a new lease on City Hall and the city itself. This enabled the organization to continue doing favors and bestowing largesse and to strengthen its hold on the city. Effective city machines proved long-lived. The precinct captain had things his way in the precinct; the ward leader controlled the ward; and the machine as a whole dominated the city. Typically, the opposition party was almost a negligible factor. There were many buyers and only one seller, and the organization did not hesitate to extract the monopoly profits resulting from its position.

The decline of machine politics in the big cities can be understood in terms of changing conditions in the marketplace. The monopoly position that the urban machine had enjoyed began to break down. Individuals needing jobs could turn to governmental employment services and no longer needed to rely on the precinct captain and the ward leader. State and local welfare organizations began to assume functions that had previously been left to the machine. As reform groups or an opposition party gained a foothold, the machine ceased to be the only means of access to the political process. With the increasing sophistication of immigrant groups there was an increasing reluctance to pay the price asked by the organization and an inclination to find, or to develop, alternative options.

Nonpartisan elections are fairly common in cities and it may appear, at first glance, that they set aside the normal processes of the political marketplace. In a nonpartisan election a candidate does not have the support of a continuing organization called a party, but he may succeed in putting together something that may serve as a temporary party. This "party" would function for a single campaign and would have little or no connection with established parties in the state. The basic market process nevertheless remains. The candidate is engaged in trying to sell products to consumers in a political market in return for their support. Nonpartisan elections do not make politics unnecessary, they simply alter the forms that political competition takes. The basic market process is not significantly altered.

In the preceding chapter the point was made that an analyst should be extremely wary about assuming a complete identity of interests between the leaders of an organization and rank-and-file members. The point is not a novel one and students of the modern corporation long ago became aware that the separation of ownership and management opened up the possibility that managers might have objectives different from, and sometimes in conflict with, those of the stockholders in a corporation. In the same way, the interests of the leader of a party may not coincide fully with the interests of rank-and-file party supporters. It requires little familiarity with political organizations or with the history of political parties to become aware that conflicts readily arise between the interests of a leader, on the one hand, and the party, on the other hand. A party leader might choose not to compete vigorously lest this competition jeopardize his organizational control. He might choose to sidetrack an issue rather than embrace it, lest the new issue attract new men to the organization who might challenge his control or his ideas. There are more than a few cases on record in which political leaders have sabotaged their party's candidate for an important office because the candidate belonged to an opposing faction. A party leader might well prefer a modest success to engaging in pitched battles that could end in catastrophe quite as easily as in a great victory. Political rhetoric notwithstanding, not all party leaders are adventurous. Sometimes, of course, the explanation for this may lie in nothing more complex than the leader's concern about the physical and emotional demands that aggressive leadership makes. The individual who commits himself to active, competitive leadership may find that he has fewer friends, more problems, and less time for his family, gardening, and poker.

# Chapter Five
# Market Analysis, Product Design, and Innovation

## Market Analysis

Political markets can be subjected to systematic analysis just as economic markets can and the techniques used in the two cases have much in common. In economics, market analysis is well-established but in politics it is quite new. The use of the public relations expert in politics is a post-World War II phenomenon and the first serious analysis of this activity did not appear until 1956.[1] The delay is to be explained largely in terms of the failure of politicians and political scientists to perceive the market aspects of politics. Because there was no body of theory explaining the role of markets and justifying market research, that activity lacked legitimacy and failed to attract attention. The need for this type of research finally became so pressing, however, that specialists began to concern themselves with it despite its lack of theoretical justification.

If the political system is to be adaptive, producers of political products must be made aware of changes in the condition of the market and in the responses of consumers to products being

[1]Stanley Kelley, Jr., *Professional Public Relations and Political Power* (Baltimore: Johns Hopkins Press, 1956).

offered. By identifying emergent wants and needs, market research facilitates the adjustment of supply and demand and contributes to system adaptation. It can also contribute to the success, or lack of it, of an individual party or interest organization. At present many of the decisions made by leaders of political organizations, even decisions of considerable moment, are based on a weak analytic foundation. It is not that these decisions are made casually or without thought but, rather, that little attention is given to gathering the kinds of information that are needed or to making the kinds of analysis that decisions should be based upon.

A marketing analyst must understand the market he is dealing with. He must locate that market and identify the characteristics of the consumers in it. He must try to find out why some persons are consuming his products and others are not and what needs to be done to convert potential buyers into actual buyers. He will want to know such things as: How closely are products inspected in the market? Is there much "comparison shopping"? What are the characteristics and appeals of competing products? What distribution channels have been proving effective? How should a new product be presented so as to maximize the prospects of consumer acceptance? How does a product acquire the status of a "brand name"?

A market analyst will want to have information upon which he can base short-term and long-term projections concerning the sales of his products. Is a given market expanding or shrinking? Are there significant numbers of consumers who will not buy his products now but who might be persuaded to buy them in another three or four years? Are the characteristics of the market changing significantly? How should his party's products be differentiated from those of other parties? He will want to have new markets and opportunities for new products called to his attention. He will be interested in estimating the elasticity of demand for particular products, that is, the magnitude of the change in demand to be anticipated in response to a given change in a product. Should a liberal candidate seek to be more liberal or less so? If a conservative candidate were more conservative would he lose support or pick up additional support? How much more? At what point would the principle of diminishing returns begin to work?

If party managers are trying to plan a campaign in a large market they will need to be aware of the fact that they will probably not be dealing with a single homogeneous market but with a variety of interlocking markets, each of which will have its own special characteristics.[2] In California, for example, one-half of the voters were not residents in the state ten years ago. California voters may therefore have a weaker sense of tradition and party loyalty than voters in other states. In every market there will be a distribution of symbol and issue sensitivities. Consumers will respond in various ways to such symbols as freedom, communism, democracy, Southerners, Catholics, Negroes, Jews, and so on. These sensitivities, and the ideological positions associated with them, represent a complex of opportunities and constraints for a political leader. He will seek to associate his organization and his candidates with attractive symbols—peace, progress, racial justice, anticommunism, or whatever. By the same token, he may try to link the opposing party with unattractive symbols—reaction, extremism, intolerance, injustice, war, and social indifference. By and large a political leader must operate within the context of the political culture that exists at a given time. He may be able to influence that culture to some extent but only, as a rule, in marginal ways.

Market research is a tool and, like most tools, it can be used for purposes that are good or bad. It can increase the responsiveness of the political and governmental apparatus to the demands of the marketplace but it can also be used by a political leader for manipulative purposes. A political leader who achieves a keen understanding of the way in which consumers act in various markets may be in a position to manipulate them to some extent. This provides another example of ways in which the needs of the system and the aims of individuals and organizations in that system may operate at cross purposes. There are some rules of the game that militate against extreme misrepresentation but there is not really a code of ethics that governs organized political behavior and there is no political equivalent of the Federal Trade

[2]One of the most interesting and imaginative studies of a political market is to be found in *Candidates, Issues and Strategies: A Computer Simulation of the* 1960 *Presidential Election,* Ithiel de Sola Pool, Robert Abelson, Samuel P. Popkin (Cambridge: M.I.T. Press, 1964).

Commission to enforce standards in political advertising. It is not yet possible to estimate the seriousness of this problem but the trend toward increased use of market research and political public relations is not likely to be reversed. If the problem should become truly serious the rules of the game may have to be formalized and extended to cover political activity in the market-place.

## Product Design

The leadership of a political party must normally produce a variety of political products—programs, individual leaders and candidates, services, stands on special issues, and an ideology. The ideology-generating process is probably less fully understood than any of the others. A party ideology normally performs a number of functions. It may or may not provide guidance for the party leaders but it certainly provides them with an instrument they can use to justify decisions and actions after the fact. It offers a simplified and attractive interpretation of party origins, the historical role of the party, and past and present stands. It explains away party errors and illuminates the errors and vulner-abilities of the opposition party. It performs a valuable public relations function by orienting individuals in the marketplace so that they will have the same frame of reference as the party leaders, will respond to the symbols wielded by the party leaders, and so on.

> Under these conditions (of uncertainty), many a voter finds party ideologies useful because they remove the necessity of his relating every issue to his own philosophy. Ideologies help him focus attention on the difference between parties; therefore they can be used as samples of differentiating stands. With this short cut a voter can save himself the cost of being informed upon a wider range of issue.[3]

> In a world beclouded by uncertainty, ideologies are useful to parties as well as to voters. Each party realizes that some citizens vote by means of ideologies rather than policies; hence it fash-

[3]Anthony Downs, *An Economic Theory of Democracy* (New York: Harper & Row, 1957), p. 98.

ions an ideology which it believes will attract the greatest number of votes.[4]

As a major party approaches an election, its leaders know that few voters will support the stand of the party on all issues. Their task is to please more voters to a greater extent than can the competing party. One aspect of this task involves determining which clusters of consumers merit particular attention. Once these clusters have been identified, special products may be designed for them. A party, therefore, does not offer a single product but a line of products. It has different products for different markets and different segments of the same market. For labor there will be a labor stand, for farmers a stand on farm income, for Negroes a stand on voting rights, schools, housing and hiring practices.

The policy stands that are incorporated in an ideology may be of doubtful consistency and the party leadership may sometimes wish that the message addressed to one group could not be heard by any of the others. If this could be arranged, the party could tailor its products to the demands of each market without concern for the overall situation.[5] This would be roughly equivalent to an economic market in which identical products are offered to different groups of consumers at different prices. As a practical matter, the high level of communication among political markets and the prominent role of the mass media makes the use of a "two-price" policy very risky. To an increasing extent what is said in one market is heard in other markets.

If a political party functioned in a purely rational way its members would design an ideology and a program incorporating that mix of elements most likely to be attractive to substantial blocs of consumers in the markets in which the party is competing. By the same token, elements in a party ideology ought to be modified at about the same tempo that the basic outlook of the electorate undergoes change. In fact, however, decisions on party ideology and party program do not result exclusively from rational calculation, although such calculation often plays a role. With the best will in the world, party leaders are apt to differ in their estimates of the way that party interests can be advanced. Propos-

[4]Downs, p. 100.
[5]See Downs, Chapter 8, "The Statics and Dynamics of Party Ideologies."

als for the use of party energies and resources will reflect varying sets of priorities, divergent ideas on strategy, and divergent alliance policies. One segment of the party leadership may believe that the party ought to invest its time, energies, resources, and prestige in supporting candidate $X$ and the program that he favors. Another may believe that an alternative plan is wiser.

The response or lack of response of a political party to change in its environment will be deeply influenced by its internal workings. The study of innovation by political parties, when it begins to be undertaken, will have to give close attention not merely to the external environment in which a party finds itself but to its internal environment as well. Party programs and ideologies may be as much the product of bureaucratic organization and internal rigidities as of rational calculation. National political parties are large, complex, decentralized organizations. They are not as bureaucratic as large commercial or governmental organizations but a trend toward bureaucratization seems clear. Managerial specialists of various kinds—professional organizers, publicists, opinion analysts, fund raisers, and so on—are now to be found in party bureaucracies. The political leaders of a party seek to work with the technicians, with a wide variety of political leaders, with party financiers, with legislators, and with various others. Party decisions emerge from the interplay of these functional groups. There is no certainty that the needs of the consumers in the market will necessarily triumph in party councils. For one thing, consumers are often not directly represented in these councils.

Nothing guarantees that the decisions that emerge from this process will necessarily advance the long-run interests of the party itself. For example, an ideology or a program may come to inspire devotion and defenders of the faith may be able to beat down challenges from those who would modify them. The program and ideology that is congenial to the powers that be in a party may be quite different from what is necessary to produce electoral victory. The products produced by a party may therefore satisfy the internal needs of a party at the expense of its external position. In other words, it is possible for political parties to produce dysfunctional decisions—they do it all the time.

Ideological and programmatic change usually does not come about because a party as a whole decides that change would be timely. It comes about because those desiring change manage to defeat those opposed to change in an intraparty contest of strength. The nominating process is often a focal point for this intraparty competition. At all political levels the nomination of candidates is of critical importance because it registers the political power of the competing factions and has an important bearing on the policies that the party will pursue for a period of time. The nominating process has the same significance for competition within the party that the election process has for competition between parties.

The prospects of a candidate for nomination will, as a rule, be heavily influenced by estimates of the marketability of that candidate. If it appears that Mr. $X$ will be an attractive candidate, he will pick up support from the backers of other candidates precisely because he looks like a winner. Conversely, if potential candidate $Y$ looks like a "loser," it will be hard for him to get the nomination since men who respect him and admire him may nevertheless give their support to $X$. If these men must choose between having a winner or having a candidate who suits them ideologically, they will often choose the winner.

This pattern is not invariable, of course. By virtue of strenuous organizational and marketing efforts prior to the convention, the supporters of Senator Barry Goldwater controlled the Republican Convention in 1964. The delegates to this convention nominated Senator Goldwater despite indications of his limited marketability as a candidate. Given a choice between a true blue conservative candidate or one with widespread appeal, they were prepared to select the former. The issue did not present itself to Senator Goldwater's supporters in quite this way, however, since many of them had persuaded themselves that Senator Goldwater was a highly marketable candidate. Their ideological attachment to the senator and what he stood for colored their judgment of political realities.

Because of the way that decisions are made in political parties, it is quite possible for contradictory elements to coexist in a party program. One group of leaders may favor one element and another a different and mutually contradictory element, and each group may be sufficiently influential to incorporate its views in the party program. The platform-making process usually provides a clear example of the importance of power considerations in party decision-making. Even then, however, rational calculation of party advantage plays a role. The more closely a party's decision-making can approximate the model of rational decision-making over the long run, the more successful the party is likely to be. With the passage of time, the capacity of political analysts to calculate the probable benefits and costs of alternative products and strategies will improve and a basis may then exist for extending the range of rational political decision-making.

Each product produced by a party will have a set of probable benefits and probable costs associated with it. In determining whether a particular new product should be introduced, political managers will want to weigh costs and benefits as carefully as they can. Some of these costs can be stated in dollar terms. The marketing of a new product may require an increase in advertising, the development of new distribution channels, an increase in personnel costs, and so on. Other costs may be associated with a loss of support. To gain the support of one element of the electorate it may be necessary to make pledges that a second element will not like. The loss of the second element's support is one of the costs involved in gaining the support of the first element. In the same way, political analysts must be conscious of the costs associated with opportunities foregone. If the choice of policy $X$ rules out the choice of policy $Y$, then part of the cost of choosing $X$ is foregoing the possibility of choosing $Y$. A thorough analysis of the costs of a particular product must include the probable returns to alternate products if they were to be chosen instead.

Since a major political party does not offer a single product but a line of products, the task of the party leadership is to design an optimum product mix. To do this with a degree of precision would require more sophisticated forms of cost/benefit analysis than are yet available. The major obstacle, of course, lies in finding statistical equivalents of the variables to be measured and in calculating gains and costs with reasonable accuracy given the limitations of human foresight.

The costs associated with a given policy or program will not normally be the same for both parties. For example, support of new civil rights legislation would create problems for the Republican party that would be quite different from those created for the

Democratic party. Because the costs are different, and the benefits as well, the two parties may not be equally eager to adopt a given policy or program. The analyst will not be able to estimate the benefits and costs of a particular policy to party *A* without making some assumptions about the expected response to *A*'s initiative from other actors, including the opposition party. If party *B* cannot follow suit, for reasons of tradition or internal politics, party *A* will enjoy unusual gains. By and large, the products that the two major parties offer on the market have a lot in common. Each party is trying to win the support of large numbers of consumers in the same national market and this dictates party policies that are not widely divergent from one another. There is, to a degree at least, substitutability of products. Because of this substitutability, the shape of the demand curve for the products of one party will depend to some extent on the actions of the competing party.

The products of party *A* will be partly substitutable for those of party *B* but not wholly so. For reasons of "party identification," some consumers will have a continuing preference for the products of one party regardless of the merits of the situation. In addition, each party takes care to see that its products are in some way differentiated from those of the opposing party. Neither party has a basis for appealing for consumer support if the products of the two parties are indistinguishable. Because the products of each party are differentiated from those of the other party a monopoly element is always present. The monopoly element is significantly modified, of course, by the fact of substitutability. Only the Ford Motor Car Company can sell Fords, but that company would be in trouble if it confused its monopoly of the production of Fords with a monopoly of the production of motor cars.

An equilibrating process is at work. Each party wants its products to be sufficiently distinctive as to be readily recognizable and to provide a basis for invidious comparison. Yet each also wants to direct its appeal to that part of the market where the most votes are to be found. If the products of party *B* are wholly unlike those of party *A* it is not likely to attract supporters away from party *A*. A nice adjustment is required so that a party's products are distinctive but not so unusual as to encounter significant consumer resistance. As noted earlier, this means that each party will tend to gravitate toward the center of the political spectrum, assuming a normal distribution of political attitudes in the marketplace.

The extent of the product differentiation between political parties, and the significance of that differentiation, will vary greatly over time. When the political situation is stable and no major social changes are afoot, this differentiation may be trivial or even spurious. Both parties will agree on the broad preferences of the electorate and neither will stray far from them. Differences in political programs will center around matters of styling and packaging. Political competition will be restricted and perhaps superficial.

If a series of new and significant problems emerge, the two parties are likely to recognize the problems and respond to them at different rates of speed and in different ways. During a time of social change, therefore, there is likely to be considerable difference in the kinds of products that the two parties offer. Product differentiation may be associated with genuine choice and innovation. During most of the 1930s the products offered by the Democrats were significantly different from those offered by the Republicans. Reform and innovation were in demand at the time and, for various reasons, the Republicans were not able to offer products to satisfy this demand. For a time, therefore, the Democratic party had a virtual monopoly of the desired political products—an enviable competitive situation. In times of change, the party that is able to innovate more easily is likely to gravitate into a position of issue leadership. Each of the major parties has exercised such leadership at one time or another.

If the new problems persist over a period of time, however, a degree of agreement is likely to emerge between the two parties on the way they should be approached. This appears to be a natural outcome of the competitive process. The approach offered by one party is likely to be more attractive than that offered by the other. In order to strengthen its position in the market, the party with the less attractive offerings is likely to modify its products so that they are more like the offerings of the other party. The process is similar to the one that leads an automobile company to follow suit when one of its competitors hits upon an unusually attractive new style or innovation. The dynamics of the competitive process point in the direction of emulation whether the market is economic or political.

## Leadership and Innovation

Decision-making in the executive, legislative and judicial branches of the government has received a good deal of systematic attention but less attention has been given to decision-making in political parties. If an observer wishes to focus on what a party does it is appropriate to treat that party as a unit. The internal reality of a party, however, is normally that of subgroups and factions contending for leadership. These factions are likely to be competing with one another with regard to such matters as strategy, tactics, candidates, issues to exploit, or whatever. The leaders of these factions compete with one another by trying to line up support for their ideas within the organization. Putting it another way, they try to sell their products (programs, candidates, and so forth) within a special market comprised of members of the party. Exchange processes are not only found in competition between parties but in competition within parties.

How do leadership and innovation emerge in this complex and competitive system? For purposes of analysis it is helpful to distinguish two types of leadership, although the distinction is often blurred in practice. One type of political leadership involves the capacity to identify the demands of the marketplace and respond to them. The other type of leadership consists of producing products that consumers have not yet learned to want and persuading consumers to want them. The latter type of leader may be thought of as a "political entrepreneur." He is not content to try to satisfy demand but wants to shape it. He is an innovator, a risk-taker who offers something new—a new doctrine, a new technique, a new perspective, a new alignment of political forces, a different allocation of political or economic resources. He seeks to get others to invest in his ideas. If he is correct in his judgments, he may reap the special "profit" that is the reward for entrepreneurship and risk-taking. This may carry him to the presidency, as in the case of Thomas Jefferson, Andrew Jackson, Theodore Roosevelt, Woodrow Wilson, or Franklin D. Roosevelt.

If he is successful, those who invest their prestige and influence in backing him are likely to be rewarded. If he is not successful those who invested in him are likely to suffer heavy losses.

A political entrepreneur may be thought of as operating on the basis of a profit motive. Profit will not be calculated in terms of dollars and cents, however, but in terms of political advantage. After all, individuals can profit in more ways than merely the financial. This means that, other things being equal, the supply of entrepreneurial leadership will be responsive to the opportunities for political profit. When the opportunities for profit outweigh the costs and the risks involved, the situation will be ripe for the exercise of entrepreneurial leadership. When the marginal returns on bold innovation are high, a large number of individuals may come forward to offer such innovation. When the marginal returns on that commodity are low, few leaders will specialize in boldness. This produces a supply curve of innovative leadership that may look like the figure below. It is important that the qualification, "other things being equal," not be overlooked. A situation might be conducive to entrepreneurial risk-taking and yet no entrepreneurs might come forward.

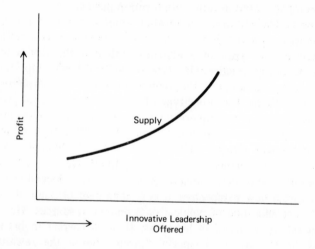

Innovation plays an important role in the American political system and deserves careful study. It could be studied much as the process of economic innovation has been studied but political scientists thus far have been slow to recognize it as a special type of political activity and one that merits close attention. Technological innovation is highly visible and its importance is likely to be apparent to everyone. Social innovation is less often perceived as innovation and its importance is often overlooked. It is a commonplace of the times to note that men's lives are being revolutionized by technological innovation, but few references are made to the way in which social innovations have revolutionized, and are revolutionizing, man's life—medicare, old-age pensions, disability payments, collective bargaining, federal aid to education, "think tanks," the United Nations, foreign aid programs, cultural exchange, NATO, the bureau of the Budget, civil disobedience, and on and on.

Innovation may take the form of a new definition of an old problem or it may embrace the recognition of a new one. It may include a suggestion for a new alliance or a proposal for a new policy or program. It may involve the raising of an issue that has been skirted, the invasion of a new market, the emergence of a new kind of leader, or the development of a new technique, skill, or institution.

Innovation can come from a variety of sources—a major political party, a minor party, an interest organization, the governmental structure, or a strategically placed individual. It is an important part of the task of many organizations to innovate. A political party will normally be concerned with innovation and product improvement. A government agency, charged with certain responsibilities, may be in the market for new ideas and better ways of doing things.

The thrust for innovation may be grounded in a variety of different motives and may be associated with the advent of a new organization, the assumption of new functions by an established organization, or with the emergence of new leadership in an organization. Innovation sometimes comes in waves, with one example giving rise to a variety of others. Market research may provide a spur to innovation if it uncovers new or strong demands, changing conditions in the marketplace, or the obsolescence of existing products. A product may be deemed obsolescent when the need that it has satisfied disappears or when that need can no longer be satisfied by that product. A common indication of product obsolescence is a decline in the number of consumers prepared to buy it.

Political parties are under pressure to develop products that will be attractive to consumers, and failure to innovate adequately can be costly. Nevertheless, innovation is often difficult. The conditions in the national market in the 1950s were very different from those of the 1930s and a number of the products that the Democratic party had marketed with notable success for two decades had become obsolescent. Nevertheless, the Democratic party continued to try to market New Deal-type products during the campaigns of 1952 and 1956.

Individuals associated with an organization usually want it to survive and prosper and hence are motivated to help it adapt. On the other hand, an organization may become so weighted down with experience of a certain kind and with vested interests that innovation becomes difficult. If a political party has been success-ful with a particular approach it may be difficult to get sufficient agreement within the party to make a change. Change almost always means risk and there will always be some to argue against any action that might "rock the boat." The *failure* of an ap-proach, on the other hand, may precipitate innovation by making evident the risks inherent in *not* innovating.

The time required for the process of innovation varies. A particular arrangement may be "sticky" and hard to change while another may be quite fluid. Sometimes circumstances will facili-tate the coming to power of the innovators and sometimes not. The speed of the innovative process may also be influenced by the extent to which the individuals concerned with innovation are self-conscious and deliberate about what they are doing. Some-time those associated with an institution will act in such a way that the institution adapts without anyone deliberately planning it. Innovation is perhaps easiest when it is not perceived as innova-tion at all as, for example, when the change is incremental and gradual. The speed of change may also depend on how great the potential gains from innovation appear to be and how certain they are. A campaign technique used successfully by one party is likely to be quickly copied by the other one. If two or three congression-al candidates run successfully on a new issue, such as pollution, that issue will soon figure in the campaigns of other candidates.

Innovation is not invariably beneficial. A political party might innovate itself right out of the market; that is, it might offer innovative products that the market is not yet ready for. Or, it might innovate in a field in which the market is approaching saturation. In 1965 and 1966, for example, President Lyndon Johnson offered more Great Society proposals than the market could absorb during a short space of time.

# Chapter Six
# System Controls

Day after day and year after year the American political system transmits information, registers wants, assesses competing influences, and grinds out political decisions. The element of command, although not absent from the system, is nevertheless of relatively minor importance. A genuine command model is seldom to be found save in an occasional smaller market such as a boss-run city. The political system as a whole is decentralized and relatively lacking in discipline. The president's power to command is limited. Except in restricted areas there is little capacity to command residing in the Congress. Political parties are loose structures and the power to command is seldom to be found there. A governor will normally pay little attention to the national leadership of his party, and the members of the state legislature belonging to his party may pay as little attention to him. And so it goes throughout the breadth of the political system.

If command does not hold the system together and keep it functioning, what does? There must be a directing or coordinating mechanism of some kind for otherwise the many moving parts would not mesh. The answer is to be found in the web of interlocking exchange processes that blankets American politics. In the absence of the power to command, the processes of adjustment and exchange occupy a central place in the system. Authority, insofar as it exists at all, emerges from bargains agreed upon by participants. The congressional leadership may agree to support several elements of the president's program in return for an informal pledge that he will not try to push legislation pertaining to other parts of his program. A governor may agree to ask for increased spending on highways provided that the state legislature will agree to pass his bills relating to education and mental health. The professional party worker exchanges his time and energy for satisfactory pay and a way of life that is attractive to him. The professional public relations man agrees to try to sell a party and its products in return for generous pay. An individual voter says, "I will vote for the party as long as it nominates candidates that are attractive and does not take stands that I find intolerable."

If exchange takes the place of command in the American political system, for the most part, what keeps the exchange system working properly? When the question is put in this way and the analyst searches the environment to find an answer, it becomes apparent that there are a number of regulatory mechanisms.

- The Market Process as a Regulatory Mechanism

Political markets in the United States are linked together. Two markets may be linked laterally by the flow of information, influence, and decisions. They may be linked by a connection with a third market, or they may be linked because both markets are incorporated within the larger national market. The flows that link political markets together are a part of the self-regulating market mechanism. They are associated with the multitudinous exchanges that take place within markets and between markets.

- Party Competition as a Regulatory Mechanism

The political party is a key institution in the American political system. Parties provide channels of communication laterally between markets and vertically between actors in the smaller markets and those in the more inclusive markets. One of the central functions that parties perform is that of knitting together the various markets. The major national parties reach across the boundaries of individual markets and provide common denominators for a vast number of them. They help make certain that consumers in the various markets are talking about the same issues. Competition between the parties also helps make the political system responsive and provides it with much of its dynamism.

Markets and parties—the two control mechanisms mentioned thus far—are closely associated. Political parties function within the framework of political markets. The working of the central market mechanism is clear. On the one hand there are consumers who have needs and are looking for products to satisfy those needs. On the other hand there are producers searching for support who offer political products as a means of attracting that support. As long as the market functions normally these two elements are mutually supportive and work together to set limits to political outcomes. If the needs of consumers are not being sufficiently met, throwing the market into temporary disequilibrium, corrective forces are set in motion. Consumer demands become more insistent as increasing numbers of consumers are affected and these demands may be given increasingly potent organizational expression. The more insistent and widespread these demands are the greater is the penalty that a party may pay for ignoring them and the greater are the rewards it will reap from trying to satisfy them. If a party fails to be receptive to these demands there will be a shift of support to the opposition party. If neither party is responsive, new political organizations may emerge that will be responsive to consumer needs. For these reasons, therefore, parties tend to stay responsive. There is nothing mystical about these "tendencies." Consumers tend to express their demands and satisfy their wants because it is in their interest to do so. Parties tend to be responsive because party leaders perceive that this is the road to success for the party and therefore for themselves. As the limits of normal operation are approached, corrective forces are brought into play. The operation of normal market mechanisms goes a long way to explain the stability and persistence of the system.

- Political Culture and Socialization

If a political market system is to work there must be a high level of voluntary support from the citizenry. Political socialization helps to generate that support. When the process of socialization is successful the values and perspectives embodied in the political culture become those of the individual. When the process works well, individuals and organizations behave in accordance with the norms and assumptions that are a part of the political culture. The political culture consists of the sum of the constitutional provisions, laws, traditions, informal rules of the game, attitudes, beliefs, and sentiments which influence the functioning of the political system. The political culture is the product of the history of the society and of the major events that have affected its political life. It includes the political ideals that are held in a polity as well as actual operating norms. The political system of the United States is embedded in the political culture of the country, so to speak, and the latter is the source of many constraints upon the system's functioning.

- The Rules of the Game

Among other things, the political culture incorporates the formal and informal rules that govern the operation of the political system. They are treated separately here simply to focus attention upon them. The formal rules consist of constitutional provisions, a body of legal decisions, relevant federal and state legislation, and municipal ordinances. They deal with a wide variety of matters including the timing and frequency of elections, conduct of campaigns and elections, the financing of campaigns, and provisions concerning residence, registration, and voting age. The informal rules include practices and understandings that regulate political behavior but which are not formal and explicit.

These rules influence the position of particular groups within the society.

> Constitutional rules are mainly significant because they help to determine what particular groups are to be given advantages or handicaps in the political struggle. In no society do people ever enter a political contest equally; the effect of the constitutional rules is to preserve, add to, or subtract from the advantages and handicaps with which they start the race. Hence, however trivial the accomplishments of the constitutional rules may be when measured against the limitless aspirations of traditional democratic thought, they are crucial to the status and power of the particular groups who gain or suffer by their operations. And for this reason, among others, the rules have often been the cause of bitter and even fratricidal struggle.[1]

[1]Robert A. Dahl, *A Preface to Democratic Theory* (Chicago: University of Chicago Press, 1956), p. 137.

The rules also influence the general working of the political system, of course, and help to provide a degree of predictability in individual and group behavior.

The rules of the game at the present time would include the following:

- Political power is legitimate only when based upon election to office. It follows, therefore, that elective office cannot be legitimately occupied by anyone who comes to it in defiance of established electoral processes;
- The political party receiving the most support in an election shall give direction to the governmental apparatus;
- Political parties are expected to compete with one another on matters of policy, program, and leadership;
- Parties may work together for certain purposes but they are not to engage in collusion that would have the effect of making the system unresponsive to changing needs;
- When parties compete with one another it shall be within the framework of normal electoral competition. Political organizations must not resort to violence, intimidation, or electoral fraud in dealing with other political organizations;
- Neither party must try to suppress the other;
- Neither party shall use governmental power or other unacceptable means to prevent the development and growth of third parties;
- Individuals shall be free to express their interests and to organize in furtherance of those interests, provided only that their agitation and activities do not interfere with the rights of others or threaten the fabric of political democracy;
- Governmental powers shall not be used by a party in power to continue itself in office beyond its appointed time. When a party is defeated at the polls it shall vacate office at the appointed time.

There are other informal rules of the game such as that a political leader should honor political debts, should be a good loser or at least look like one, and should not be ruthless in suppressing intraparty debate. Rules of this kind are part of the political culture but they are less basic and the penalties associated with their transgression are not severe or certain.

At any given moment the rules of the game can be thought of as fixed, whether they are written into law or have an informal status. From a longer perspective, however, they can be seen to be evolutionary. In time, as the political culture changes, it generates new norms and rules. Rules that were controversial may cease to be so. Rules that were changeable may become firm, and those that were firm may become infirm or pass from the scene altogether. Changes in the rules of the game are most likely to be rapid when the society as a whole is undergoing rapid change and when there are significant shifts in the relations between powerful groups. The rules of the game reflect, to some extent, the power arrangements that exist at a given time. Major changes in the power relations of groups are likely to lead to demands for changes in the rules. Before the Civil War the rules of the game tolerated slavery and the formal denial of the right to vote to large numbers of Negroes. The rules governing the political participation of Negroes were drastically transformed in the 1960s. Until 1920 the rules of the game also denied the vote to women.

One of the rules that has long been honored is that decisions made in accordance with the established legal and political processes shall be adhered to even by those who opposed them before the final decision was made. If one did not like a law, one was free to try to change it; but one was not free to disobey it or to oppose its execution by obstruction and violence. This informal rule also had formal legal status. During recent years, however, it has been undergoing modification formally and informally. Civil rights groups have engaged in various forms of protest and civil disobedience. Disobedience, arrest, and courting of a jail sentence have been deemed to be legitimate and effective ways to call attention to laws considered unjust. Similarly, opposition to the war in Viet Nam has been expressed by acts of civil disobedience—burning of draft cards, obstruction of military recruitment, refusal to serve in the armed forces, and so on. Civil disobedience, long unacceptable, and an exotic growth on the American political scene, has become commonplace. The frequency with which it has been resorted to has given it a quasilegitimate status.

The rules of the game, formal and informal, have a great impact upon the functioning of the political system. The functioning and the evolution of that system, in turn, have a substantial impact upon the rules of the game. More broadly, if the political culture provides the immediate context within which the political system operates, the political system also has an impact upon the political culture. In its operation it affects the values, expectations, and preferences of individuals and, by so doing, alters the political culture. The political culture is also modified by other influences, of course, such as the changing pattern of life, the problems that a society faces, and the victories and defeats that it encounters. It must not be forgotten that the political culture is a part of a larger culture. The political system will be influenced by developments in that larger culture, therefore, as well as by those in the political realm. Changes in the larger culture usually transmit themselves to the political system via the political culture, however.

## Sanctions and Obligations

There are two broad types of sanction that support the rules of the game and ordinary market transactions: extralegal sanctions and legal sanctions. Individuals act in accord with the norms of the political system because they believe in those norms and/or because they do not wish to risk the disapproval of those who do believe in them.

Trust plays an important role in the American political system. In the absence of legal obligation, it is often trust and the desire to merit trust that leads participants to honor informal obligations. The literature on politics written by practicing politicians emphasizes the importance of gratitude, loyalty, and trust. These virtues help keep the system going.

Since a reputation for trustworthiness is often a valuable political asset, it may be worth considerable effort on the part of an actor to acquire and retain such a reputation. This may require a scrupulous observance of agreements and informal understandings, even when it is disadvantageous, in the short run, to do so. An actor in a market customarily engages in repeated transactions rather than a single one, and the way he behaves in one transaction is apt to be remembered to his advantage or disadvantage in subsequent ones.

If the level of trust and confidence among actors is low, the threat of sanctions is likely to be important. Each actor may threaten to take reprisals against the other in the event of non-compliance. Reprisals may take any of a variety of forms depending upon the circumstances. An actor may refuse to collaborate with another in the future, may throw his support in an alternative direction, may seek to destroy the other's reputation for honor and trustworthiness, and the like.

One of the characteristics of transactions in political markets is the frequency with which they generate unspecified obligations. It is not uncommon for actor *A* to do something for *B* in the expectation of a return, but the nature of the return and the date of payment is left up to *B*. Obligations of this kind have been central to the functioning of many city organizations. A ward leader may pay the bail for one constitutent and find a job for another without a word being said about any kind of repayment. He can afford to leave the transaction open-ended because he is confident that his constituents know how to repay him without being told. This kind of knowledge is an established part of the political culture and may be taken for granted. Even if every individual does not fulfill his tacit obligation to the ward leader enough of them will do so to make this type of activity worthwhile to him. The same sort of calculation appears to underlie the readiness of congressmen to engage in errand-running for their constituents.

To say that basic rules of the game are strongly adhered to in the United States is not to say that every individual will adhere to them under all circumstances. An individual might be in favor of the rules in an abstract sense and yet be unaware that some of the policies he favors contravene those rules.[2] It means, rather, that when the issues are fully understood and the conflict is perceived, there will be a strong presumption on the part of most individuals toward adhering to the rules of the game. Political leaders do not imprison the leaders of the opposition, close

[2]See James W. Prothro and Charles M. Grigg, "Fundamental Principles of Democracy: Base of Agreement and Disagreement," *Journal of Politics*, vol. 22 (March, 1960), pp. 276–294.

down opposition newspapers, assassinate leaders of the opposition, nor seek to retain office despite losing an election—and voters would immediately cease to support them if they did. These things are not an accepted part of American political practice, and the knowledge that they are not helps create a reliable set of common expectations for those participating in the political process.

Individuals and organizations careless of the rules of the game run the risk of severe public reaction. Textbooks in American history have never forgiven the Federalist party for passing the Alien and Sedition Acts in an effort to impede the emergence of the Jeffersonian Republicans. The Federalists were not playing the game—even though the basic rules of the game were just emerging at that time. An organization such as the Ku Klux Klan sometimes uses violence and gets away with it, but it weakens its claim to legitimacy by so doing. In a society that does not approve of the use of organized violence by private organizations, the more attention the Klan calls to itself by its violence the more likely it is that it will be ostracized or that formal action will be taken against it.

Legal sanctions are important to the political system but probably less important, on the whole, than extralegal sanctions. Some transactions are legally enforceable, as when an organization contracts for the services of an individual or a firm, but many are not. If a voter believes a candidate's pledge to bring honesty and efficiency to city hall and supports him, he has no recourse to the courts if the official fails to live up to his pledges. On the other hand, if it can be established that the official has engaged in corrupt practices that is another matter and legal action can be taken.

Congress and the state legislatures play a role in connection with the rules of the game. If they choose to, they can convert certain informal rules into binding legal obligations which the executive agencies and courts must enforce. The power to investigate, involving as it does the power to publicize, is also a potent weapon in encouraging compliance with the rules of the game. The courts have played a role in connection rules having to do with voting rights. A few nongovernmental organizations such as the American Civil Liberties Union have also played a role in helping to support the rules.

The men who drafted the Constitution sought to fashion a political system that would be held in bounds by an elaborate set of checks and balances. If the president tried to make himself too powerful he would quickly discover the powers that had been given to Congress. If the Congress sought to dominate the executive branch it would soon learn the potency of the presidential veto. Each house of Congress would check the other, the powers of the federal government would be checked by those of the states, and so it was to go. The framers were thinking in terms of command and of specific injunctions. They took it for granted that if the network of checks and balances broke down the entire system would fly apart. These checks and balances did not work as intended—and yet the system did not fly apart.

The framers of the Constitution had great faith in formal rules of the kind they wrote into the Constitution. These proved to be quite unreliable, however. The day was saved by the existence of self-regulating mechanisms which they did not plan for, and by self-restraint, which they would have had little confidence in. They did not foresee the development of a political culture and the extent to which individuals would be socialized into compliance with its values and informal rules. An important part of the explanation for the perpetuation of the American political system is therefore to be found in those elements which the Founding Fathers either did not understand or would have lacked faith in: the market system; the party system; an evolving political culture; and an evolving set of formal and informal rules of the game.

# Chapter Seven
# Political Change
# and the Market System

Thus far in this book the American political system has been treated as if it were relatively changeless. Or, more precisely, attention has been focused on those features of the system associated with its normal operation. A political system is not fully understood, however, until its functioning in time of crisis and change can also be explained. Political scientists have been hampered in their efforts to explain political *change* in the United States because they have lacked a theory that would explain the system's *normal* functioning. The advent of a crisis does not miraculously transform the system. The basic elements remain the same; they simply interact in ways that are different.

Since the central feature of the political system during its normal operation is the political market, one might anticipate that the factor that would throw the system into a crisis mode of functioning would be a malfunction in the market process. In this chapter a theory of political crisis will be offered that revolves around the working of the national political market and that seems to be in accord with historical events. At this juncture it must necessarily be somewhat speculative however.

As noted in Chapter One, a series of flows are associated with the functioning of a political market. The inflow of political products is the "supply" available to the market while the outflow of support represents the "demand" that has been satisfied by those products.

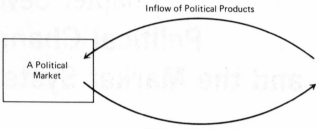

Outflow of Political Support

Products flow toward the market at varying rates, through a number of different channels and from a variety of sources. Because of imperfections in the distribution process, the quantity of products supplied to a market in a given period will rarely be the same as the quantity produced. Within the market, resources of one kind are exchanged for resources of other kinds. Through a series of exchanges, almost any resource can be exchanged for almost any other resource. A political concession might be exchanged for increased financial support, electoral support, or something else.[1]

A "sale" by one individual or organization is, at the same time, a "purchase" by some other individual or organization. Sales and purchases offset one another because they are simply different aspects of the same set of transactions. As the market systems to be analyzed become increasingly complex it will be helpful to keep this characteristic of market processes in mind: Total sales always equal total purchases.

There is a two-way flow into and out of the market. Political products flow into the market from organizations and support flows back to those organizations from the market. Support flows from the market in a variety of forms, through a large number of

[1]Each party to a transaction is both a producer and a consumer. Candidates and political organizations "produce" political products and "consume" the support that they get in exchange for those products. Constituents, on the other hand, "consume" political products and "produce" political support. Although the discussion in this work focuses primarily upon the *production* role of candidates and organizations and the *consumption* role of constituents, it will be helpful to bear this duality of roles in mind.

channels to a number of different destinations. The flow of products into the market need not equal the outflow of support, however, because supply and demand rarely offset one another exactly. (Demand and "consumption" are not identical, of course, for demand can exist without being satisfied by consumption.)

The diagram below indicates the multiple sources of products, the varied channels through which they reach the market, and the varied channels through which political support flows out of the market and back to the major political parties.

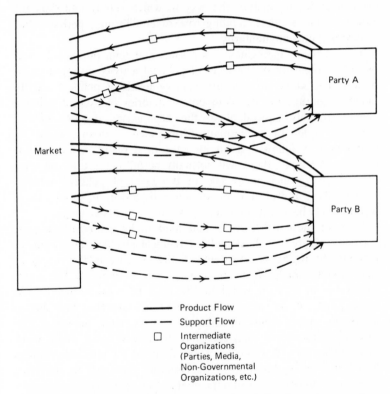

Product Flow
— — Support Flow
☐ Intermediate Organizations (Parties, Media, Non-Governmental Organizations, etc.)

This analysis draws attention to six analytic elements: production; supply; demand; sales; purchases; and consumption. The means for measuring all of these quantities are not yet available but, hopefully, as in the case of national income statistics, ingenuity will not be long in developing a set of measurements once the need for them becomes clear and a body of theory exists that can put the resulting data to work. Each of these variables is capable of aggregation and each of the aggregates so produced will be related to each of the others, directly or indirectly. Taken together, these aggregates should allow the political analyst to examine many questions that would otherwise be out of reach, including those pertaining to major political change. A political market, when it is working properly, will be characterized by processes of equilibration and mutual adjustment. The use of these aggregates, and the construction of supply curves and demand curves, should make it easier to analyze the way in which supply and demand adjust to one another, tending toward equilibrium, perhaps, but achieving it only momentarily.

Two of these aggregates—total sales and total purchases—will provide a measure of the level of political activity during a given period. The ability to measure varying levels of political activity might encourage the development of theories of cyclical political activity roughly equivalent to the economist's theories of the business cycle. In preliminary form, such a theory might be formulated as follows: If an increase in demand is met by an increase in supply, there will normally be an increase in the level of exchange, which is to say, in the level of political activity. Conversely, if a drop in demand is met by a drop in supply, there will normally be a reduction in the level of political exchange.

Each of these processes would tend to be self-reinforcing, at least to a degree. If the supply of political products increased, in response to an increase in demand, the increase in the supply of new products might elicit a further increase in demand. The result would be an upward spiral in the level of political activity. At some point, of course, demand would be saturated and an increase in supply would elicit no further demand increases. The upward spiral would then cease. A downward spiral might work in a similar way. If a decline in the demand for political products led to a drop in the supply, the resulting reduction in attractive options available to consumers might lead to a loss of consumer interest and to a consequent further drop in demand.

It should be emphasized that there are many levels of political activity at which the system might be thoroughly stable. If the demand for new products were high, the system would be stable as long as there was a high level of supply of those products. If the demand for new products were low, the system might be stable with a low level of supply. In short, if supply and demand are properly adjusted, system stability is compatible with either a low level or a high level of political activity. There is probably a floor, however, below which demand would not normally sink. Even in a stable and prosperous society there will continue to be a flow of demands of one kind and another. The existence of such a flow places a lower limit to the level of political activity that can be expected.

In this explanation of cyclical changes in the level of political activity, demand is the dynamic factor. To have an impact on political activity, domestic and foreign influences must first have an impact on demand. Autonomous changes in supply might initiate small shifts in the level of political activity, but in seeking to explain major cyclical movements in the level of political activity it seems safe to concentrate on demand.[2]

Supply and demand are central features in the normal functioning of the political system; they are also central features in the crisis functioning of the system. When the political system functions normally, supply and demand adjust to one another. In these circumstances it is not too much of an oversimplification to say that demand plays the key role, since so many of the factors that affect the market·exert their influence initially through the modification of demand. Demand may be influenced by changes in transportation, communication, swings in the domestic economy, ideological shifts, events on the world scene, and so on. Structural factors may also affect demand—factors such as an increase in the number of consumers, changes in the average age of consumers, an increase in the number of organizations on the political scene, and an increase in the size and wealth of such organizations. Changes in the formal rules of the game, the informal rules, and the control mechanisms of the market will benefit some groups and hurt others and, in the process, lead to altered demands. Demand is also modified as new issues emerge

[2]To date political scientists and historians have evinced little interest in trying to identify cyclical swings in political activity. However, see Walter Dean Burnham, "The Changing Shape of the American Political Universe," *The American Political Science Review*, vol. LIX (March, 1965), pp. 7–28.

periodically in the market. The emergence of new groups or changes in the aspirations of established groups will also normally lead to the articulation of new demands.

Small and unobtrusive cumulative changes may, over a period of time, have as great an influence on demand as the dramatic and more obvious factors. Not all types of change lead to demands for modification, however. Slow changes in the size of the electorate, gradual modification of the economy or the communications system, for example, may not lead to new demands, but may modify the functioning of the system or its environment in subtle ways without ever being made the focus of attention by parties or leaders in that system.

If demand holds the key to the functioning of the political system during its normal operation, supply holds the key to its crisis operation. It is the failure of supply that plunges the system into crisis. Any number of circumstances may contribute to this failure. Demand may remain unsatisfied because it has not been brought forcibly to the attention of decision-makers or because products capable of satisfying it have not been developed. It may remain unsatisfied because the products that would satisfy it are not acceptable in the market area. Or powerful elements in society may be able to block needed innovation. Seemingly unimportant procedural arrangements in the governmental apparatus may, under some circumstances, prevent the system from being responsive. For example, a strategically located congressional committee chairman may be able to block badly needed legislation. Supply may be unresponsive if neither party feels driven to innovate because of fear of competition from the other. If the major parties are immobile and a third party is prevented from coming into existence supply may be unresponsive. Sometimes, of course, it may be beyond the capacity of the political system to satisfy the demands being made upon it. This might be the case if the discontent had to do with international affairs or threats from other nations.

When supply fails to respond to demand, unrequited demand is produced, that is, demand unsatisfied by available products. If the level of unrequited demand is low it means that the system is working fairly well. If the level is high, it means that supply is not adjusting very well to demand and represents a danger signal. As the level of unrequited demand begins to climb, several consequences may be expected. For one thing, discontent and anger will be generated. Second, consumers, unable to find products that satisfy their wants, will begin to consume the products of the major parties at levels far below normal. Associated with this is likely to be the formation of interest groups and organizations or possibly a new party. Negro discontent in the 1960s led to the formation of a variety of new organizations and student discontent led to the formation of organizations such as the SDS (Students for a Democratic Society) and the Liberation News Service.

As the level of unrequited demand rises beyond the normal range, the political system is subjected to increasing strains. Demand is likely to assume a progressively more revolutionary aspect. At some point the political system may be said to have departed from its normal mode of functioning and to have entered a crisis mode of operation.[3] Whenever the political system moves into a crisis mode of functioning, systemic breakdown becomes a possibility. Another alternative is, of course, that supply may finally respond to demand and the system will once more pass into its normal mode of operation.

In 1786 the unrequited demands of hard-pressed farmers and debtors in Massachusetts led to Shay's Rebellion. The danger of civil war seemed very real at the time. "There are combustibles in every State which a spark might set fire to," wrote George Washington. "I feel infinitely more than I can express for the disorders which have arisen. Good God! Who besides a Tory could have foreseen, or a Briton have predicted them?" In 1860 unrequited demand led to secession and Civil War. In 1877 the first great industrial conflict in the history of the nation took place. In Baltimore, Pittsburgh, Chicago, San Francisco, and other cities there were battles between the militia and mobs of strikers and unemployed. Federal troops were required to restore order. The decades of the 1880s and 1890s were punctuated by serious disturbances such as the Haymarket Riot, the Homestead Strike and the Pullman Strike. The Panic of 1893 saw "General" Jacob Coxey lead an army of unemployed on Washington. During these decades the political system was slow in accepting and adjusting to the emergent demands of labor, the unemployed, and the

[3]For a discussion of the circumstances under which political cleavages may be particularly severe see Part Three of Robert Dahl's *Pluralist Democracy in the United States* (Chicago: Rand McNally, 1967).

socially and economically depressed. In the early 1930s, the unrequited demands of a significant proportion of the population generated powerful explosive forces. In each of the cases mentioned above, the crisis was caused by the failure of supply to keep pace with demand. In each of these situations, to be sure, supply ultimately did respond, the crisis was overcome, and the political system returned to its normal mode of functioning.

The events of the late 1960s also exemplify the explosive potential of unrequited demand. During this period the dissatisfaction of many blacks with the American political system reached the boiling point. They felt that they had been making demands for years but the system had not responded to those demands, or had responded in a slow and inadequate way. Many wondered if the system was rigged against them in such a way that it never could respond to their demands. As faith in the responsiveness of the political system declined violence and riots became more common. The inability of the political system to satisfy Negro demands and its slowness in responding to the demand for an end to the war in Vietnam led to widespread civil disobedience and violence and to a disruption of life on many college and university campuses. This, in turn, led to a militant and repressive response and to increasing political polarization. By the end of the decade of the 1960s the sense of demoralization and crisis was general.

The capacity of a society to innovate in response to emerging demands is vital to its stability. If the level of unrequited demand in that society is high, it may be ready for rapid and far-reaching innovation. If it is low, on the other hand, the rate of innovation will have to be slow.[4]

[4]The necessary research has not been done to establish the characteristics of the innovation function for this society, but the curve might look like the following:

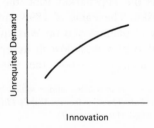

Innovation

Important to any theory of political innovation is the willingness of voters to cross party lines. Will voters accept innovation only if it appears in the party to which they are attached, or are they willing to consume attractive new products offered by the other party? One of the most reliable characteristics of American political behavior appears to be the potency of party identification. About 85 percent of American voters express some degree of party preference and about one voter in three will express strong party preference. If a large percentage of voters are locked into parties by their party preferences, how can political parties be the instruments by which the political system adjusts to changing needs? Given the strength of party preferences, how can the innovative party be rewarded for its adaptability?

First, it is clear that those voters who are not locked into political parties *can* shift. Since national elections are commonly decided by a few percentage points, small shifts can be significant. Next, a shift of votes or public sentiment toward party *B* may persuade the leaders of party *A* to introduce products similar to those offered by *B*. The system would be adjusting because both parties had responded to demand, even if not simultaneously.

In time of great crisis, however, the process of adjustment might be quite different. There is evidence that substantial numbers of voters have altered their party loyalties in time of crisis. As a consequence of loyalty shifts during the Civil War and Reconstruction, the Republican party became the majority party in the nation and remained so for over sixty years. During the Depression crisis of the early 1930s there was another massive shift in party loyalties which resulted in the Democratic party replacing the Republican party as the stronger of the two, a predominance which held for over three decades.

Party allegiance, which is stable during quiet times, may become unstable during times of domestic crisis. When the ground underfoot becomes shaky, voters turn to those leaders, and to that party, offering action. During the Depression crisis this reaction affected even leaders of the Republican party.

> Summoned by the new President (Roosevelt), Congress convened in special session on Thursday, March 9. While Freshman members were still looking for their seats, the two houses hastily organized and received a presidential message asking for legisla-

tion to control resumption of banking. The milling representatives could hardly wait to act. By unanimous consent Democratic leaders introduced an emergency banking act to confirm Roosevelt's proclamation and to grant him new powers over banking and currency. Completed by the President and his advisers at two o'clock that morning, the bill was still in rough form. But even during the meager forty minutes allotted to the debate, shouts of "Vote! Vote!" echoed from the floor. "The house is burning down," said Betrand H. Snell, the Republican floor leader, "and the President of the United States says this is the way to put out the fire." The House promptly passed the bill without a record vote; the Senate approved it a few hours later; the President signed it by nine o'clock.[5]

Elections that come at such times are different from normal elections. A normal election proceeds within the framework of existing party loyalties. A crisis election, on the other hand, is likely to be marked by the malleability of established party loyalties. If new products are offered on the market—new leaders, new programs, new approaches, new legitimacy symbols—the constraints of party loyalty will be sharply reduced and party lines will be crossed with an ease that would not be seen during normal times.

Party identification should not be thought of as a constant, therefore, but as a factor that varies with the degree of sensed crisis. Perhaps, at the beginning of a crisis there is little effect on party allegiance. At some point, however, a threshold may be passed and party loyalty may suddenly become fragile. As the crisis deepens, increasing numbers of voters are likely to conclude that other values may be more important than party loyalty.[6]

[5]James MacGregor Burns, *Roosevelt: The Lion and the Fox* (New York: Harcourt, 1956), pp. 166–167.

[6]The characteristics of the party identification function have yet to be determined but the curve may have a kink in it.

Shifts in Party Identification

When the political system functions normally there is a fairly high degree of ideological convergence between the major parties. In a time of crisis, however, there is likely to be a substantial degree of ideological divergence and a corresponding amount of product differentiation. Leaders in the two parties are not likely to be equally bold, imaginative, and receptive to new ideas. They are not likely to be equally capable of moving their parties along new lines of policy. Furthermore, the party that was in power while the crisis deepened is likely to have a vested interest in defending the way things have been done. The party out of power may find it easier to take a fresh look at the situation and to propose changed policies.

The preceding chapter discussed the formal rules and informal norms that govern the behavior of actors in the market system. The rules discussed were those which apply when the system is functioning normally. During times of domestic crisis the growing polarization in the body politic is reflected in the debate over rules. The rules of the game cease to be taken for granted and deviation from them becomes increasingly common. Those who deviate are insulated from the disapproval of society as a whole by the strong and vocal approval of their own immediate reference group. The rationale for such deviation may be that the rules are not really those of society as a whole but rules developed by a special segment of society to meet their own needs and protect their special position. "It's your system not our system, and you run it in accordance with your rules to satisfy your own interests." When an element in society becomes disaffected and concludes that the system is structured in such a way as to be completely unresponsive to its needs and to the problems that it faces it is likely to lose respect for the system, for the rules by which it operates, and for the specific decisions which it produces. Devotion to the democratic principle will not long survive if the system based on that principle produces results that are consistently unfavorable in the eyes of a particular minority.[7]

When an important element in society feels that the normal channels of political action are closed to it its leaders may explore new means of expression such as civil disobedience, harassment, and violence. Since a key rule of the game forbids violence and

[7]See Kenneth J. Arrow, *Social Choice and Individual Values* (New York: Wiley, 1951), pp. 90, 91.

intimidation, a debate, of sorts, over the rule is inevitable. Those favoring the rule argue that violence is not necessary because the political system is responsive to demands for change that are expressed through normal channels. Those opposing the rule argue that the system is *not* responsive and that that is why violence is both necessary and justified. Instead of being almost universally condemned, political violence develops its own rationale. It is depicted as a means to the achievement of social justice. It is also argued that violence is in keeping with the democratic spirit since it is simply a way of forcing the political system to do what it should be able to do without the spur of violence. In an effort to legitimize violence its proponents may point out that America has a long and rich tradition of political violence going back to the Boston Tea Party and the Revolution itself. "Violence is as American as apple pie."

How does a society select the problems that it is prepared to deal with? An easy answer is that it deals with the problems that are "important" to it. But how does it determine what is important? There are a great many problems at hand at a given moment but a society chooses to perceive some as important and others as not important.[8] Nothing guarantees that problems will receive attention in proportion to their intrinsic gravity. Minor problems may receive speedy attention while grave problems may be ignored or neglected for decades. Conditions can persist for a long time before they come to be defined as serious problems. All of the following have, to at least some extent, been "discovered" as problems within recent years: poverty in America; hunger in America; crime and violence; the problems of the cities; the quality of life in the cities; the problems of the ghettos; racial strife; the problems of the high schools; students and universities; and the ecological crisis. Doubtless other problems will be discovered in fairly rapid succession.

A problem may be identified initially by the dispassionate analysis of experts but it is not likely to be elevated to the status of an "important" problem, that is, a problem about which something really needs to be done, until numerous persons or powerful interests are affected by it. Those persons affected by the problem

---

[8]For an interesting discussion of this and related questions see Albert O. Hirschman, *Journeys toward Progress* (New York: Twentieth Century Fund, 1963), Chapter 4.

seek to call attention to their concern by using a variety of channels: pressure groups, contact with executive agencies, communication with congressional figures, communication with party leaders, and publicity programs. If the persons affected by the problem have little access to decision-makers through normal channels then decision-makers are under no pressure to perceive the problem as important and it may therefore go unrecognized. Poverty and hunger in America were not new, but their being perceived as problems was new. The poor and the hungry were not formerly in a position to call attention to their needs. Those needs did not begin to be recognized until leaders organized dramatic and unorthodox actions such as a poor people's march on Washington.

Using the elements discussed above, the onset of a political crisis may be presented schematically as follows:

1. Demands are made on the political system by powerful or numerous elements in the society.
2. For one reason or another these demands are not met by an increased supply of political products.
3. The failure of supply generates unrequited demand.
4. As unrequited demand persists over a period of time it comes to be associated with reduced levels of political consumption and increases in discontent and anger. Political organization is likely to emerge among those who feel disadvantaged.
5. Unrequited demand increases sharply.
6. There is an increasing degree of polarization within society and an increasing amount of disagreement on the utility and justice of the rules of the game.
7. There is an increased reliance on violence and a deepening sense of crisis.
8. As the level of unrequited demand rises and the sense of social malaise also increases, an increased readiness to accept innovation will be found among various elements in the society.
9. New organizations may come into existence in order to advance the needs of those who feel that the political system is slighting their needs. A minor party may be started.

10. The growing sense of crisis will weaken voter attachments to particular parties. Voters will become increasingly ready to give their support to any party that appears ready to take effective action in dealing with pressing problems.

11. Responding to demand, party $X$ offers a series of new products and quickly attracts new support. This action by party $X$ introduces a high degree of product differentiation between the products that $X$ is offering and those that party $Y$ is offering.

12. New products are also offered in other parts of the political system such as Congress and the Executive Branch.

13. These new products and proposals, which would have seemed radical only a short time before, no longer seem extreme. There is a shift of support from party $Y$ to party $X$.

14. As a consequence of this shift party $X$ assumes office. If party $X$ was already in office its hold on power is consolidated.

15. The nature of political intercourse has been noticeably changed. New policies and programs have come into being. New political alliances have been formed. The issues and problems being discussed are not the same as they were earlier, and the political attachments of voters have been significantly altered.

16. The level of violence declines sharply.

17. The sense of crisis wanes. Interests are no longer perceived as being irreconcilable. The rhetoric appropriate to common interests replaces that appropriate to combat and zero-sum games, and moderate leadership emerges to replace militant leadership.

18. The process of normalization picks up momentum: unrequited demand begins to decline; the propensity to accept innovation returns to a normal level as does the propensity to shift party allegiance.

19. Party $Y$ accepts the changed circumstances and begins to offer products quite similar to those of party $X$. Product differentiation, so important a short time before, returns to normal levels.

20. The rules of the game, modified in procedural and other ways, once more win broad acceptance and become a guide to behavior.

The cycle of crisis change is now complete and the political system has returned once again to its normal mode of functioning. Supply, having precipitated the crisis in the first instance by its failure, initiates the recovery process by its belated response. The time for radical innovations and new departures is past. Consumers are locked into their new party attachments, perhaps for the next two or three decades. With the decline in the extent of product differentiation, the two-party system now functions once again in its accustomed way.

For purposes of presentation in this chapter, the crisis operation of the political system has been sharply distinguished from the system's normal operation. In practice, the distinction will not always be sharp. The political system may be subjected to varying degrees of strain and may approximate the crisis mode of functioning to a greater or lesser extent. It should also be stressed that change and innovation are not confined to the crisis mode of operation. There is change during the normal operation of the system as a continuing flow of products is developed to meet a continuing flow of demands.

# Chapter Eight
# Democracy and the Market System

## Government and the Market Process

The party system and the governmental system are intertwined in many ways. Therefore an analysis of party competition reveals some of the dynamics of governmental response as well. In a strict sense, to be sure, it is not a party's response to demand that is important to consumers but the government's response. A political party cannot pass a bill. Only Congress can do that. It may not be the president as party leader who satisfies a demand, but the president as Chief Executive. This book is primarily concerned with competition between parties, however, and can touch only glancingly on the market aspects of the national government's functioning.

The federal government has a powerful influence on both the demand and supply sides of the market. By its actions it can encourage the expression of demands by various segments of the population. It is also a major producer of political products. It is the recipient of a continuing flow of demands and whenever it responds to a demand it affects the supply of political products. Its products are produced by all three branches and may take a variety of forms—a tax cut, modification of a social security program, payments to farmers, modification of the tariff, direct subsidies to an industry, a judicial decision, an administrative ruling.

Incoming demands may be received at many points in the governmental structure. They may be received by the federal courts, by administrative agencies, by individual congressmen or congressional committees. When these demands are received in the legislative and executive branches they are processed in one way or another. Important demands may require interagency and congressional action. A relatively minor demand, such as a request for a favorable administrative ruling on some matter, may be handled within a single agency. A congressman may introduce a bill at the request of a group of his constituents and that will be the end of the matter. He has produced a product that satisfies the constituents' demand, and by satisfying that demand he has presumably won additional political support.

Those individuals who sit in Congress won contests in markets called congressional districts. When they get to the legislature they will discover that they have entered a new market, a market in which many buyers and sellers interact, in which many products are offered, and in which transactions take place that have an impact upon the entire nation. The processes of bargaining and exchange that take place in Congress are similar, in some respects, to those taking place in other markets. Congressional committees are offered draft legislation originating in interest groups, in other committees, or in the Executive Branch. The Executive Branch is not always a single seller when it approaches Congress. Competing products may be offered to a committee by competing agencies or even by competing elements in the same agency. Military officers in the Defense Department, for example, may sometimes push programs that are at odds with the recommendations of their civilian superiors. If a committee accepts a particular bill, it then becomes a product that the committee tries to sell to other committees and to the Congress as a whole. If the members of that committee cannot find the necessary minimum number of buyers for the bill in its original form, they may be willing to modify the product in order to attract additional buyers.

The Executive Branch as a whole and individual agencies can also usefully be analyzed in terms of market processes. Supporters of various proposals seek to sell those products to other agencies in interagency negotiation. Competition, bargaining, buying, and selling take place. As in other markets, the final outcome can be analyzed in terms of who bought (or did not buy) what and what price was paid by whom to whom.

## Democracy and the Political Market

It is the market process that gives the American political system those features that allow it to be termed a democracy. It follows, therefore, that the breakdown or impairment of the market process would involve the breakdown or impairment of democracy in the United States.[1] If the market process is central to the functioning of the American political system then a number of the questions that have occupied democratic theorists should be restated or reexamined in terms of market analysis.

Democracy is usually discussed and analyzed in either/or terms. A political system is deemed to be democratic or undemocratic. If it is not one it must be the other since those two alternatives exhaust the possibilities. This is rather like arguing that if perfect competition does not exist in an economic market than there is no competition at all. In Chapter VI the essential rules for the functioning of a political market were set forth. Several of those rules are clear-cut and allow little room for uncertainty. For example, the defeated party must leave office at the appointed time and failure to do so would mean that democracy had broken down at that point. Other provisions, however, admit of degree. There must be party competition, but how vigorous does this competition have to be to satisfy minimum standards? There must be "periodic" elections, but how frequent must they be?

These questions suggest that there may be variations in the *degree* to which democracy may be said to exist. Democracy can be thought of in scalar terms. The more fully each of the individual requirements is satisfied the more fully democratic a political system may be said to be. This perspective makes it clear that a

[1]There is a rich literature on democratic theory only a few titles of which can be cited here: Robert A. Dahl, *A Preface to Democratic Theory* (Chicago: University of Chicago Press, 1956); Giovanni Sartori, *Democratic Theory* (New York: Praeger, 1965); Neal Riemer, *The Revival of Democratic Theory* (New York: Meredith, 1962); Anthony Downs, *An Economic Theory of Democracy* (New York: Harper & Row, 1957); Charles E. Lindblom, *The Intelligence of Democracy* (New York: Free Press, 1965); and *The Federalist* (any edition).

system may fall short of being thoroughly democratic (that is, satisfying each of the requirements to a high degree) and yet may offer workable democratic arrangements. The minimum requirements for a working democracy are far less demanding than those for a thoroughgoing democracy.

It has not been easy for democratic theorists to relate the role of leaders to the role of the people in a democracy. Rule by the people was manifestly unachievable but rule by an independent elite was unacceptable. If an observer understands the market process, however, he is not faced with the question, "Who rules, the people or the leaders?" Instead, he will be aware of the transactional nature of American political life, the part played by the political culture and the rules of the game, the multiplicity of political markets, the extent to which decision-making is fragmented, and the competition among different elites. The market approach recognizes the importance of political elites but sees that these competing elites must win support in the political marketplace.

Another question relating to democratic theory has to do with the rationality of the individual citizen. Critics have argued that democracy is vulnerable because voters do not have the rationality that democratic theory imputes to them. On what basis, they ask, can the rationality of the voter be defended in view of: the low level of information possessed by many voters; the extent of political apathy; the impact of public relations on politics; the low level of analytic ability evinced by many voters and the relative lack of coherence among the ideological and information elements possessed by them; the increasing complexity of public issues; and the tempo of social change, with the attendant rapidity in the obsolescence of ideas and information.

The argument is similar to the one sometimes made by economists when they consider the ignorance of the consumer in an economic market. The consumer, they point out, does not know what he is getting, does not have a laboratory to test the medicines, automobiles, or washing machines that he is buying, and does not even try to engage in comparison shopping before making his market decision. The response to these observations is that the market process, despite the ignorance of many consumers, nevertheless works fairly well. Some social processes can work reasonably well despite the imperfect nature of the human material with which they deal.

Economic markets do not need "perfect" consumers and political markets do not require perfect citizens. The achievement of a workable democracy does not require a high level of information and rationality among citizens. It is not asking very much of the individual to express discontent, to make demands, and to make a choice among competing political organizations. Furthermore, it is not even required that *all* individuals perform these functions in order that the system work passably. Only a substantial number of individuals are needed. High levels of rationality, information, and involvement are desirable and will improve the working of the political system but they are not essential to the maintenance of a stable, working democracy.[2] The proof of the assertion lies in the fact that a working democracy has been maintained in the United States for over a century and a half despite the varying levels of rationality, knowledge, and involvement that have prevailed during that period.

The central organizing principle of a political system will shape and influence a great many characteristics of that system. This is true, for example, of the type of authority found in the American political system. Authority is not based upon hereditary right, the possession of military power, the godlike qualities of a leader, or a doctrine that asserts a mystical right to rule on the part of a particular party. It is not based on a succession of orders from an authoritative source that commands compliance. Instead, authority derives from the outcome of market processes. Political actors behave as they do because the myriad exchanges that take place in political markets generate an almost infinite number of obligations, tacit or explicit, of a quasicontractual nature. The rewards

[2]"*Individual voters* today seem unable to satisfy the requirements for a democratic system of government outlined by political theorists. But the *system of democracy* does meet certain requirements for a going political organization. The individual members may not meet all the standards, but the whole nevertheless survives and grows. This suggests that where the classical theory is defective is in its concentration on the *individual citizen*. What are undervalued are certain collective properties that reside in the electorate as a whole and in the political and social system in which it functions." Bernard R. Berelson, Paul F. Lazerfeld, William N. McPhee, *Voting* (Chicago: University of Chicago Press, 1954), p. 312.

and punishments that the system provides are such that these obligations are fulfilled most of the time.

Economic markets rely upon self-interest as a driving force and the same is also true for political markets. It is perceived self-interest that leads consumers to press their demands and to throw their support to parties and interest groups that most nearly appear to satisfy those needs. It is self-interest that leads parties to compete with one another in trying to satisfy consumer demands. The market system could not work without self-interest but, at the same time, it is deeply influenced by the side effects of the working of the self-interest principle.

The system tends to be more sensitive to problems and concerns based on self-interest than those that are not. The reason for this is evident. Producers respond to demands that are made upon them. The most reliable source of these demands is self-interest. Therefore producers devote most of their time to satisfying the demands of self-interest. If a program or need can find self-interested support or opposition it is assured of attention. If a need cannot arouse such support or opposition, it is likely to be overlooked, however important it may be by some external standard.

This characteristic of the market helps explain why the political system has so much difficulty planning ahead. The market is sensitive only to present, felt needs. If a future danger or future problem does not find a concerned constituency *now*, it will probably be ignored. If a problem or a change has only begun to emerge on the horizon and the majority of voters do not *now* see it as promising significant rewards or penalties, they will pay little attention to it. Because they are not concerned with it, they make no demands and do not respond to products that are offered dealing with it. Therefore nothing much is likely to be done.

This same characteristic of the market process helps explain why the system, historically, has been relatively unresponsive to community needs, whether defined in national, regional, or local terms. Most community needs are not such that they can attract and hold a large self-interested following.[3] Those who are op-

---

[3]"Benefits from many government actions are remote from those who receive them, either in time, space, or comprehensibility. Economic aid to a distant nation may prevent a hostile revolution there and save millions of dollars and even the lives of American troops, but because the situation is so remote, the

posed to satisfying these needs often find it easy to enlist the support of small but ardent groups of self-interested backers. Handsome highways are built—and are then defaced with countless billboards and filling stations. Industrial development often proceeds with little attention to community concerns such as air pollution, water pollution, and traffic problems. Companies may move into a community and build commercial structures with little concern for the appearance of the community or its style of life.

The *laissez-faire* ideology, as it has commonly been understood in economic marketplaces, teaches the individual that it is appropriate for him to pursue his self-interest with little heed for the public interest because the rational pursuit of private interest results in the advancement of the public interest. In political life, on the other hand, few have been bold enough to argue that an invisible hand guarantees that the pursuit of private interest automatically advances the community interest. The evidence is overwhelming that the pursuit of special interests by small minorities may easily interfere with the public interest, as in the case of a small minority blocking the passage of effective gun control laws. When an individual (or a political organization) makes a political decision he is not making a decision that affects only himself and therefore his personal interest cannot properly be his sole standard of judgment.[4]

---

average citizen—living in rational ignorance—will not realize he is benefitting at all. Almost every type of preventive action, by its nature, produces such hidden benefits. People are not impressed with their gains from water purification, regulation of food and drugs, safety control of airways, or the regulation of utility and transport prices, unless these actions fail to accomplish their ends. Then, perhaps for the first time, the absence of effective protection makes them aware of the benefits they were receiving when it was present.

In contrast, the immediate benefits of almost all private goods are heavily emphasized. In order to sell these goods on a voluntary basis, the producers must convince the public of their virtues. Thus consumers are subject to a continuous advertising barrage stressing the joys of private goods, whereas no comparable effort dramatizes the benefits they receive from government action. Even private goods with benefits of a remote nature, such as cemetery lots, are advertised in such a way as to make awareness of these benefits immediate." Anthony Downs, "Why the Government Budget Is Too Small in a Democracy," *World Politics*, XII (July, 1960), pp. 551, 552.

[4]See Henry Oliver, "Attitudes toward Market and Political Self-Interest," *Ethics*, LXV (1955), pp. 171–180.

As noted above, producers tend to respond to market demand, and demand is usually grounded in self-interest. To be sure, there are some types of demand in the marketplace that are not grounded in self-interest. For example, there are often public spirited individuals who are deeply concerned with the broad development of a community. However, their numbers are likely to be few, their efforts sporadic, and their accomplishments disappointing. As a day-in and day-out motivating force in politics, public spirit tends to be a poor match for self-interest.

Although most of the demand in a political market will be generated by self-interest, not all self-interest generates demand. This is another characteristic of the political system that needs to be noted. Nothing forces the system to be responsive to needs that are not urged in the marketplace. It *may* be responsive under certain circumstances but it need not be. Needs must be translated into "demand" before the political system will begin to process them. This means that the needs of inarticulate minorities or groups of consumers, however great, may be ignored if they do not also have the capacity to punish or reward in the political market. The various groups of immigrants that entered American cities did not receive much attention until each organized itself to intervene in the political process. For decades the interests of those living in the slums or ghettos received little attention because those interests were not translated into effective political "demand." The drive for Negro voter registration in the South was based on the realization that the system will be far more responsive to Negro needs if Negroes become a major factor in Southern political markets.

As long as the political system in the United States is organized on the basis of political markets it will continue to have the kind of problems referred to above. In some cases these problems can be ameliorated however. Since the system has trouble responding to the needs of the inarticulate and the unorganized, greater emphasis can be placed on early and effective organization of these elements. Since the system has trouble responding to certain kinds of community needs perhaps more can be done to educate individuals in that respect and perhaps the political culture will come to confer greater status on community activities. Since the system has trouble planning ahead, perhaps more citizens can be educated to see the present implications of problems that have not yet fully emerged. The political system relies heavily on open lines of communication and access for its effective functioning—and these lines are not always open. Their openness can always be examined, however, and can be improved if it is found lacking. Political parties play an important role in the system but are imperfect instruments. Their market analysis is inadequate; they are slow to perceive opportunities and to innovate; they do not plan well, do not examine alternatives as carefully as they should, and utilize overly simple strategic ideas. However, all of these features are capable of being altered.

The competitive functioning of a market will be impaired to the extent that it is dominated by producers, by consumers, or by a producer-consumer alliance. The self-regulating supply and demand mechanism will then have ceased to work. However, if it is normal for a consumer group or a producer to try to control a market, it is also normal for other units in the market to resist the extension of that control. It is in the interest of individuals living in that particular market area (town, city, state, nation) that competitive market processes not be replaced by monopoly. A motivational basis and an organizational basis therefore exists for self-correcting tendencies within the market.

Despite its imperfections the American political system has worked fairly well over its life span. It has been reasonably innovative and responsive. Demands that have been able to find expression in the marketplace have been listened to, as a rule. Competing interests have been accommodated fairly well. The policy outcomes that the system has generated have usually been accepted as "legitimate." Because a multiplicity of groups have been able to participate in the decision-making process and because the decision-making process itself is thought to be fair, the system has attracted a high level of compliance. The network of political exchanges and the strength of the informal sanctions has meant that relatively little force has been necessary to keep the political system running. The discontent of special interests and minorities has seldom become explosive and, with the exception of the Civil War, there have been few serious attempts at the armed overthrow of the government. The political system makes use of highly complex communications and signaling systems. Yet these complicated and interlocking systems manage to work, utilizing the frail and imperfect human material that is at hand. The market process is well-adapted to the pluralism of American life. Many elements in society are able to have an impact upon political outcomes but no one element has been able to dominate governmental policy across-the-board over a period of time. The United States has never known tyranny at the national level and it has never known extreme instability. The many semiautonomous political markets in the country are also valuable to a democratic society. These markets are linked together with varying degrees of intimacy but they also have a degree of autonomy as well. These multiple power centers help the American political system preserve its pluralist character.

To say that a political system works fairly well and is reasonably responsive to the demands of the electorate is not to say, of course, that it will consistently produce just or rational results. It will produce results that are responsive to the demands of the marketplace—and these may be just or unjust.

# Appendix
# Political Competition: Thoughts on an Agenda for Research

There are many phenomena that analysts of the American political system would like to be able to explain and to link together but cannot. The field is still in search of a theory. There is some micro-theory but not much in the way of macro-theory and very little that ties the micro and macro levels together so that the system as a whole can be analyzed, using a set of consistent and complementary concepts. The chances are that much that is going on in the political system is lost on contemporary observers because they lack a set of theories and analytic concepts to aid their perception. In any realm of investigation, observers usually fail to see those things they are not looking for. Political science is very conscious at present of being oriented toward the study of political behavior, but this does not mean that *all* significant forms of political behavior are being studied. Those forms of political behavior are being studied that observers are aware of and to which they attribute significance. Behavior that they are not aware of or to which they attribute little importance is not studied.

It is not premature to begin trying to develop macro-theory dealing with the American political system. If there is any political system about which quantitative data is available it is this one. The market approach outlined in this volume offers one way to attack the problem of developing macro-theory. It conceives of resources flowing through the system, being combined with other resources, and being converted and exchanged. It also gives prominence to the processes of perception, communication, and bargaining, as any satisfactory macro-theory of the political system must. It encourages observers to ask a different range of questions than they have been accustomed to ask and it does relate macro- and micro-analysis. At the macro level the analyst can inquire about market structure, market processes, the state of competition in a market, and so on. At the micro level he can investigate the way that an organization analyzes its marketing situation, how it designs and markets its products, how it makes its decisions. Many of the concepts that would be applied to the analysis of interparty competition can also be applied to intraparty competition.

Macro-theory implies the need for a set of political aggregates and the market approach offers a set of such aggregates. Before long the political analyst may have at his disposal a family of interrelated aggregates that he can manipulate—total production, total supply, total demand, total sales, total purchases, and total consumption. These aggregates, or others related to them, may in time prove to be as powerful as the aggregates that the economist has at his disposal such as gross national product, net investment, total consumption, total investment, and others. Measures of flows through the political system need to be developed but it is still too early to be sure which flows will prove to be most important or how some of these measurements are to be used.

The market approach to the study of American politics points toward a number of new areas for research and toward the establishment of new research priorities. There needs to be a systematic study of political markets and the relations between markets.[1]

More needs to be learned about coordination among markets and the way in which the communications and signaling systems work. Complicated self-regulatory mechanisms are involved and

[1]"We encourage others to analyze the many alternative substantive exchange markets since, in our view, this is the next great field for theoretical advance in political science." R. L. Curry and L. L. Wade, *A Theory of Political Exchange* (Englewood Cliffs, N. J.: Prentice-Hall, 1968), p. 55.

their working is little understood as yet. Techniques need to be developed for examining the structure of political markets and for tracing changes in structure over a period of time. Political leadership and influence are bound to appear in a somewhat different light when they are examined in the context of political markets and exchange processes, as are the concepts of "power," "authority," and "influence." It would be helpful to know more about the way in which political parties adapt to varying market situations— a static market, a shrinking market, an expanding market. Does behavior tend to be more aggressive and noncollaborative in one case than another? Would it be possible to develop some rough decision-rules that would help explain and predict the outcomes of party decision-making?

Analysts of political processes need to have a better understanding of bargaining and the ways in which the terms of political exchange are agreed upon. What are the normal formalities of bargaining? What kinds of things are likely to be explicitly communicated in bargaining and what things tacitly? How common are those exchanges in which the participants never communicate explicitly but in which each has a clear idea of what is being exchanged for what? In some cases the understanding may be simply: "If you don't raise issue $X$, we won't raise it either." More needs to be known about the way in which bargaining processes may vary from one market to another and from one type of negotiation to another. How does bargaining between equals differ from bargaining between a strong actor and a weak actor, and how does political bargaining change if there is only one seller in a market rather than two or more? What conditions promote stable exchange relationships? What factors tend to impede exchange—confusion, ignorance, mistrust, communications failures, differences of interest?

Very little attention has been paid thus far by American political scientists to the study of variations in political activity. There is no body of political thought that corresponds to the economists' concern with business cycle theory. What are some of the ways in which variations in levels of political exchange can be measured and what are some of the factors that help explain these variations? What are the conditions which promote political stability and how do they differ from the conditions which encourage innovation? What can be learned about the conditions under which new demands emerge? What sorts of things have led to important changes in the political culture and in the rules of the game?

The approach to the study of the American political system that is stressed in this book, with its emphasis on markets and transactions, should make easier the achievement of an integrated politicoeconomic analysis of American life. The political and economic aspects of national life are clearly intertwined but at present the analysis of one tends to proceed independently of the analysis of the other. As long as the concepts used by the economist and the political scientist are as different as they have been no real synthesis is possible. The market approach gives promise of closing the gap to some extent. Perhaps, in time, a major politicoeconomic synthesis may be feasible. The market approach may also be of some value for the purposes of comparative political analysis.

An important area for research should be that centering around an analysis of the imperfections in the functioning of the political system and in the development of recommendations for improvement. Political scientists have no systematic way of evaluating the functioning of the political system and are therefore not in a position to make recommendations about heading off trouble nor about what to do when trouble arises. Political scientists need to develop a set of questions which, when answered, will allow them to know how the political system is functioning and what should be done to improve it: What is the level of political activity? Is the political system stable? Is it innovating at an adequate rate? Is it allocating resources in accordance with pressing needs? Are healthy competitive conditions being maintained in its major markets? It may well be, for example, that if healthy competitive conditions are to be maintained in political markets, political equivalents of the antitrust laws will have to be developed.

# Bibliography

ARROW, KENNETH J., *Social Choice and Individual Values*. New York: John Wiley & Sons, 1951.

BANFIELD, EDWARD C., *Political Influence*. New York: The Free Press, 1961.

BARRY, BRIAN, *Political Argument*. New York: Humanities Press, 1965.

BAUMOL, WILLIAM J., *Welfare Economics and the Theory of the State*. Cambridge: Harvard University Press, 1952.

BLACK, DUNCAN, *The Theory of Committees and Elections*. Cambridge: Cambridge University Press, 1958.

BLACK, DUNCAN, and R. A. NEWING, *Committee Decisions with Complementary Valuation*. London: William Hodge, 1951.

BLALOCK, HUBERT M., *Toward a Theory of Minority-Group Relations*. New York: John Wiley & Sons, Inc., 1967.

BLAU, PETER, *Exchange and Power in Social Life*. New York: John Wiley & Sons, 1964.

BOULDING, KENNETH, *Conflict and Defense*. New York: Harper & Row, 1962.

BOWEN, HOWARD, *Toward Social Economy*. New York: Holt, Rinehart and Winston, 1948.

BRETON, ALBERT, "A Theory of the Demand for Public Goods," *Canadian Journal of Economics and Political Science*, XXXII (November, 1966), pp. 455–467.

123

124    *Competition in American Politics*

BUCHANAN, JAMES, *Fiscal Theory and Political Economy*. Chapel Hill: The University of North Carolina Press, 1960.

———, "Individual Choice in Voting and the Market," *Journal of Political Economy*, LVII (1954), pp. 334–343.

———, "An Individualistic Theory of Political Process," *Varieties of Political Theory*, ed. David Easton, pp. 25–37. Englewood Cliffs, N. J.: Prentice-Hall, Inc., 1966.

———, "Positive Economics, Welfare Economics, and Political Economy," *Journal of Law and Economics*, II (1959), pp. 124–138.

———, *The Public Finances*. Homewood, Ill.: Richard D. Irwin, 1960.

———, *Public Finance in Democratic Process*. Chapel Hill: The University of North Carolina Press, 1967.

———, "The Relevance of Pareto Optimality," *Journal of Conflict Resolution*, VI (December, 1962), pp. 341–354.

———, "Social Choice, Democracy, and Free Markets," *Journal of Political Economy*, LXII (April, 1954), pp. 114–123.

BUCHANAN, JAMES, and GORDON TULLOCK, *The Calculus of Consent: Logical Foundations of Constitutional Democracy*. Ann Arbor: University of Michigan Press, 1962.

BUCHANAN, JAMES, and M. Z. KAFOGLIS, "A Note on Public Goods Supply," *The American Economic Review*, LIII (June, 1963), pp. 403–414.

CASSTEVENS, THOMAS W., "A Theorem about Voting," *American Political Science Review*, LXII (March, 1968), pp. 205–207.

CATLIN, GEORGE E. G., *The Science and Method of Politics*. London: George Allen & Unwin, 1927.

———, *A Study of the Principles of Politics*. London: George Allen & Unwin, 1930.

———, *Systematic Politics*. Toronto: University of Toronto Press, 1962.

CHAMBERLAIN, NEIL W., *A General Theory of Economic Process*. New York: Harper & Row, 1955.

COLEMAN, JAMES S., "Foundations of a Theory of Collective Decisions," *The American Journal of Sociology*, LXXI (May, 1966), pp. 615–627.

COLM, GERHARD, "Theory of Public Expenditure," *Annals*, CLXXXIII (January, 1936), pp. 1–11.

COMMONS, JOHN R., *The Economics of Collective Action*. New York: The Macmillan Company, 1951.

COSER, LEWIS, *The Social Functions of Conflict*. Glencoe, Ill.: The Free Press of Glencoe, 1956.

CURRY, R. L., and L. L. WADE, *A Theory of Political Exchange*. Englewood Cliffs, N. J.: Prentice-Hall, 1968.

DAHL, ROBERT A., and CHARLES E. LINDBLOM, *Politics, Economics, and Welfare*. New York: Harper & Row, 1953.

DOWNS, ANTHONY, "In Defense of Majority Voting," *Journal of Political Economy*, LXIX (April, 1961), pp. 192–199.

————, *An Economic Theory of Democracy*. New York: Harper & Row, 1957.

————, *Inside Bureaucracy*. Boston: Little, Brown, 1967.

————, "Why the Government Budget Is Too Small in a Democracy," *World Politics*, XII (July, 1960), pp. 541–563.

DYE, THOMAS, *Politics, Economics, and the Public*. Chicago: Rand McNally & Company, 1966.

GAMSON, WILLIAM A., *Power and Discontent*. Homewood, Ill.: The Dorsey Press, 1968.

GARVEY, GERALD, "The Theory of Party Equilibrium," *The American Political Science Review*, LX (March, 1966), pp. 29–38.

HEAD, JOHN G., "Public Goods and Public Policy," *Public Finance*, XVII (1962), pp. 197–219.

HINES, LAWRENCE G., "The Hazards of Benefit-Cost Analysis as a Guide to Public Investment Policy," *Public Finance*, XVII (1962), pp. 101–117.

HIRSCHMAN, ALBERT O., *Journeys Toward Progress*. New York: The Twentieth Century Fund, 1963.

HOMANS, GEORGE C., "Social Behavior as Exchange," *The Journal of Sociology*, LXII (May, 1958), pp. 597–606.

————, *Social Behavior: Its Elementary Forms*. New York: Harcourt, Brace & World, 1961.

HOTELLING, HAROLD, "Stability in Competition," *The Economic Journal*, XXXIX (1929), pp. 41–57.

JOHNSON, CHALMER, *Revolutionary Change*. Boston: Little, Brown & Company, 1966.

LINDBLOM, CHARLES E., *The Intelligence of Democracy: Decision-Making through Mutual Adjustment*. New York: The Free Press of Glencoe, 1965.

LINDBLOM, CHARLES E., and DAVID BRAYBROOKE, *A Strategy of Decision*. New York: The Free Press of Glencoe, 1963.

MARCH, JAMES G., "The Business Firm as a Political Coalition," *Journal of Politics*, XXIV (November, 1962), pp. 662–678.

MARGOLIS, JULIUS, "A Comment on the Pure Theory of Public Expenditure," *Review of Economics and Statistics*, XXXVII (November, 1955), pp. 347–349.

MAY, K. O., "A Set of Independent Necessary and Sufficient Conditions for Simple Majority Decisions," *Econometrica*, XX (October, 1952), pp. 680–684.

MITCHELL, WILLIAM C., *Sociological Analysis and Politics*. Englewood Cliffs, N. J.: Prentice-Hall, 1967, Chapter 4.

———, WILLIAM C., "The Shape of Political Theory to Come: From Political Sociology to Political Economy," *American Behavioral Scientist*, XI (November–December, 1967), pp. 8–37.

MUSGRAVE, RICHARD, *The Theory of Public Finance*. New York: McGraw-Hill, 1959.

OLIVER, HENRY, "Attitudes toward Market and Political Self-Interest," *Ethics*, LXV (1955), pp. 171–180.

OLSON, MANCUR, *The Logic of Collective Action*. Cambridge: Harvard University Press, 1965.

PARSONS, TALCOTT, *Sociological Theory and Modern Society*. New York: The Free Press, 1967.

PENNOCK, ROLAND, "Federal and Unitary Government—Disharmony and Frustration," *Behavioral Science*, IV (April, 1959), pp. 147–157.

POLANYI, MICHAEL, *The Logic of Liberty*. Chicago: University of Chicago Press, 1951.

RIKER, WILLIAM, *The Theory of Political Coalitions*. New Haven: Yale University Press, 1962.

———, "Voting and the Summation of Preferences: An Interpretative Bibliographical Review of Selected Developments during the Last Decade," *American Political Science Review*, LV (December, 1961), pp. 900–911.

RIKER, WILLIAM, and PETER C. ORDESHOOK, "A Theory of the Calculus of Voting," *American Political Science Review*, LXII (March, 1968), pp. 25–42.

RIKER, WILLIAM, and RONALD SCHAPS, "Disharmony in Federal Government," *Behavioral Science*, II (1957), pp. 276–290.

RIORDEN, WILLIAM L., *Plunkitt of Tammany Hall*. New York: Knopf, 1968 (originally published in 1905).

SAMUELSON, PAUL A., "Diagrammatic Exposition of a Theory of Public Expenditure," *Review of Economics and Statistics*, XXXVII (November, 1955), pp. 350–356.

———, "The Pure Theory of Public Expenditure," *Review of Economics and Statistics*, XXXVI (1954), pp. 387–389.

SCHATTSCHNEIDER, E. E., *The Semi-Sovereign People*. New York: Holt, Rinehart and Winston, 1960.

SCHNEIDER, EUGENE V., and SHERMAN KRUPP, "An Illustration of Analytical Theory in Sociology: The Application of the Economic Theory of Choice to Non-economic Variables," *The American Journal of Sociology*, LXX (May, 1965), pp. 695–703.

SHUBIK, MARTIN, "Approaches to the Study of Decision-Making Relevant to the Firm," *Journal of Business*, XXXIV (April, 1961), pp. 101–118.

STIGLER, GEORGE J., "The Tenable Range of Functions of Local Government," *Federal Expenditure Policy for Economic Growth and Stability* (Washington, D.C.: Joint Economic Committee, 1957), pp. 213–216.

TULLOCK, GORDON, "Entry Barriers in Politics," *American Economic Review: Papers and Proceedings*, LV (May, 1965), pp. 458–466.

————, (ed.), *Papers on Non-Market Decision Making*. Charlottesville, Va.: Thomas Jefferson Center for Political Economy, University of Virginia, 1966.

————, *The Politics of Bureaucracy*. Washington, D.C.: Public Affairs Press, 1965.

————, "Reply to a Traditionalist," *Journal of Political Economy*, LXIX (April, 1961), pp. 200–203.

————, *Toward a Mathematics of Politics*. Ann Arbor: University of Michigan Press, 1967.

THIBAUT, JOHN W., and HAROLD H. KELLY, *The Social Psychology of Groups*. New York: John Wiley & Sons, 1959.

TIEBOUT, CHARLES M., "A Pure Theory of Local Expenditure," *Journal of Political Economy*, LXIV (October, 1956), pp. 416–424.

WILLIAMS, ALLEN, "The Optimal Provision of Public Goods in a System of Local Government," *Journal of Political Economy*, LXXIV (February, 1966), pp. 18–33.

WILSON, JAMES Q., and EDWARD BANFIELD, "Voter Behavior on Municipal Public Expenditures: A Study in Rationality and Self-Interest," *The Public Economy of Urban Communities*, ed., Julian Margolis, pp. 74–91. Baltimore: The Johns Hopkins Press, 1965.

ZETTERBERG, HANS L., *On Theory and Verification in Sociology*. Totowa, N. J.: The Bedminster Press, 1963.

# Index